I0818854

AMMI'S KITCHEN

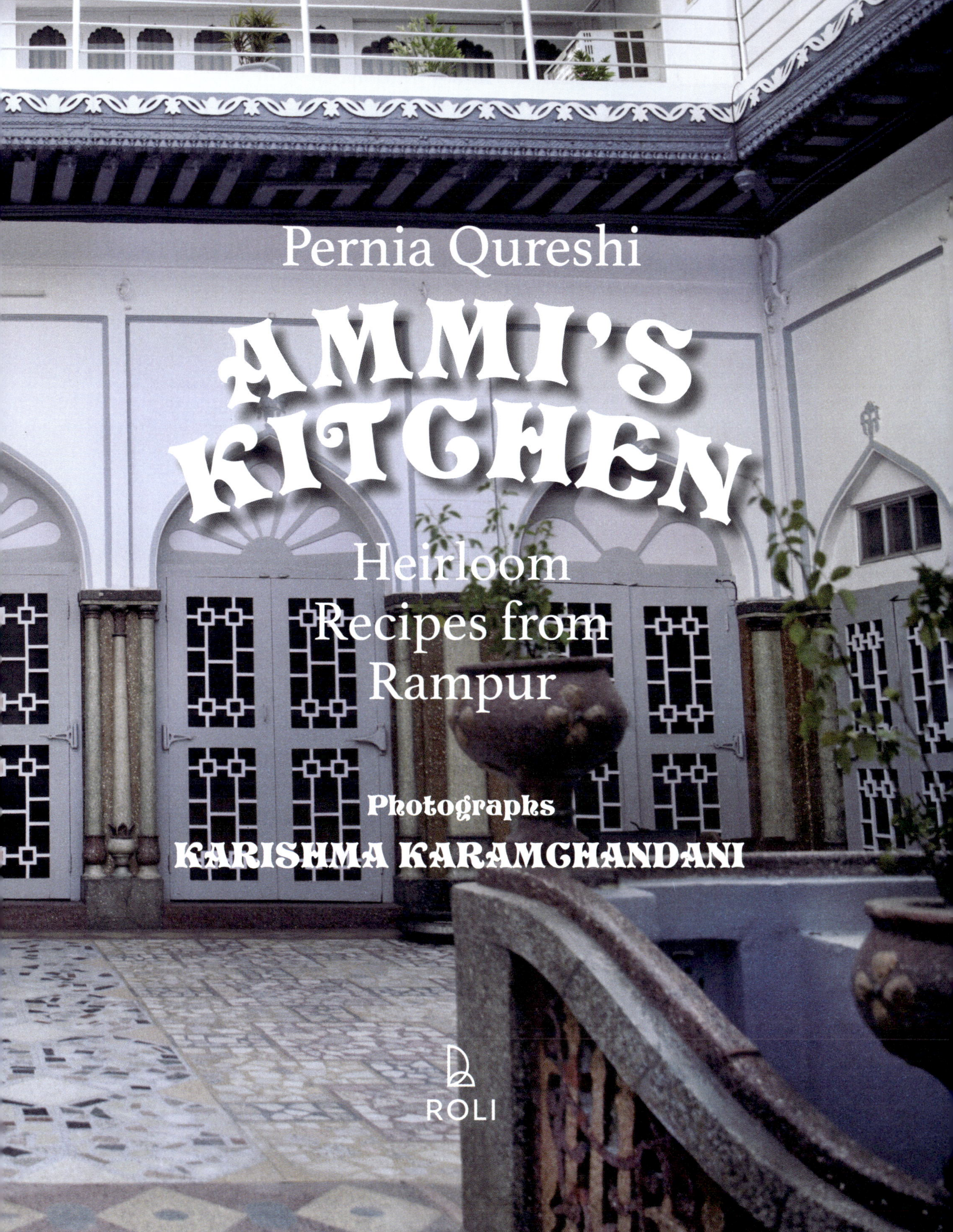

Pernia Qureshi

AMMI'S KITCHEN

Heirloom Recipes from Rampur

Photographs
KARISHMA KARAMCHANDANI

ROLI

CONTENTS

INTRODUCTION

Musharraf Begum's beginnings were humble. She was from a small town in Uttar Pradesh called Chandausi. Due to the financial hardships faced by her family, they agreed to marry her off to a rich, much older gentleman from Rampur as his fourth and only surviving wife then. To this day, the tales of how my grandfather's first three wives died are vague and come in several versions. One story goes that my grandfather's wife was travelling to him on a ship after the nikah and they were caught in a storm where she passed away. The bottom line was that here was this nobleman with the worst luck when it came to his wives, so much so that no established family was willing to marry their daughter to him. The 'jinxed' Abdul Majeed Qureshi had to then seemingly settle for a fair, young uneducated girl from a family that was in desperate need of his financial support. She would later boast that she was chosen based on her beautiful hands and feet since that was all her in-laws saw before her marriage was arranged.

Soon enough, her staff, children and townspeople began to call her Ammi – a moniker she earned early on, likely because of the authority she wielded at home and in the kitchen. Around 1946, when she was a young new bride who had entered Rampur, a princely town much bigger than what she was used to, she had a lot to prove and a significant role to take on. Her biggest assets proved to be her passion for food and her ability to cook. As women of her generation often did, she controlled the kitchen, and her dazzling personality began to reflect in her food. With the influences of her hometown mixed with her newfound exposure to Rampur's more modern cuisine, Ammi created a food language that was uniquely her own. For instance, *keema khichdi*, a meal in itself made by slow-cooking mutton keema with rice and spices and eaten with a cube of yellow butter, cold dahi and mint chutney, is one of our most popular household staples, and has its origins in Chandausi.

From fabrics and borders to frames – a trunk full of beautiful memories of my Ammi.

When Ammi just got married, a young boy was employed in the kitchen named Israil Bhai who went on to become her sidekick and together they created magic. I can still hear them bantering over why something was missing from the fridge and Ammi calling him *tokri ke* (basket case), as the most terrible insult she could muster because it was her worst-kept secret that he was too dear to her to rebuke him seriously. Despite a fairly large kitchen, they would often set up a *choolah* (stove) outside, using bricks and wood to slow-cook dishes. With eight children and several grandchildren, there were always people to feed. Cooking and eating seemed to be the central point of Ammi's world. Be it hosting *daawats* (feasts) on behalf of her husband for the Nawab and itinerant dignitaries, or a *langar* or family wedding, Ammi's kitchen was always feeding.

Ammi's portion of the house dating back to the 1800s was called the dalaan *in Persian, which translates to verandah, and was her reception area.*

Rampur cuisine, with its infusion of Mughlai, Awadhi and Afghani influences, when combined with Ammi's sensibilities and the Chandausi culture, resulted in a rather mutton-heavy offering. When most think of Rampuri cuisine, the first dishes that come to mind are kebabs like *seekh* and *chapali*. But, for me, the most representative Rampuri dish is our family staple *taar gosht*—mutton cooked in a masala gravy where the ghee is meant to be so generously used that when you dip your roti in it, there should be a *taar* (line) of ghee connecting your bite to the plate. Ammi used *taar gosht* as her go-to dish for all occasions, whether it was a wedding or a funeral. To her, the dish was

rich enough that no one could criticize her for not doing enough while also satisfying the large appetites of our food-loving people.

Another reason Ammi was an exceptional cook was that she was extremely adaptive. Due to my grandfather's ill health in his later years, he was advised to eat light meals. Together, they used to travel to Calcutta frequently and Ammi quickly picked up how to make lighter, British dishes for him during her stints there. This was the best thing about her—food was her love language. She knew exactly who needed and loved what in her family. By 2010, she was living with us in Delhi and every time I would come back from a trip, I would magically have my favourite *gobi gosht* with *bina happa* (black dal khichdi) on the table for lunch. She was also the queen of combinations. She knew exactly the dishes that complimented one another—knowing instinctively to pair a *kaddu bharta* with a *pyaaz ki sabzi* and *besan* roti—the perfect summertime meal with just the right balance of flavours. Even now, we don't dare to switch out any of her combinations.

(Left): The green wall and picture frame – the colours and motifs, the smells – everything about Ammi's house transports me back to another time. (Centre and far right): The beautiful mosque in our neighbourhood in Rampur was built by my grandfather, who also built a school for the community. The buildings endure even today.

In 1997, when my family opened the Rampur Kitchen—a restaurant in Delhi's Khan Market, meant to bring our cuisine to tables in our capital, Ammi and Israil bhai personally arrived to train the chefs in the recipes of our kitchen, like the chapli kebabs and the chicken kaali mirch. The food soon garnered a cult following, with lines around the block even for takeaway orders.

With our family, Ammi wielded the same authority as she did in the kitchen. My best memories of her in Delhi include her sternly telling me off for counting my rotis and watching my diet, of her taking my *nazar* off almost daily, kissing her head while she prayed namaz, and finding her in splits with my sister over family gossip.

During that golden period of our lives, my sister, Sylvia, had the brilliant idea of starting a home food delivery business for Ammi. We thought it would be something she would enjoy, and it would keep her occupied, but it became so much more than that. Ammi became an entrepreneur at the age of ninety. Sylvia would take the orders and Ammi would do everything else. From arranging for groceries to overseeing the cooking and packaging, she was immersed. She would put her earnings of the day in a pouch and sleep with it under her pillow. It often made me think that with her talent, charm and elephantine memory, Ammi would be ruling the world if she was given the opportunity.

Nothing like an authentic Rampuri meal cooked in clay ovens and brick stoves.

She lived to be close to hundred years old and passed on this talent and passion for cooking to two of my aunts and my father. During the Covid lockdowns, my father had the opportunity to truly indulge in his first love, food. He perfected the softest chicken seekh kebab, and after many tests, the best shoestring fries. Like his mother, my father's love language, too, I

noted, was cooking and feeding. During my recent pregnancy, when the doctor asked me to up my protein intake, he made me at least twenty-five variations of eggs. Incidentally, Israil bhai, too, passed on his love for food to his son, Mazhar, who has now taken over the kitchen in our family home with a practiced familiarity from growing up having watched Ammi and Israil bhai at it.

As spoilt as we are with the best when it comes to what we eat, I worry about the culinary legacy of my family after my parents' generation. So far, Ammi's recipes have been preserved through oral histories because there were people in the family with the same passion for cooking as Ammi, people who wanted to keep her traditions alive. This book is my gift to future generations of the family, so they can feel Ammi's love in their lives even though she is no longer with us. The greatest inheritance we have from her is her recipes, which are wrapped in all her love and memories. This book is also for everyone belonging to Rampur and Chandausi, so that they can have a piece of their home wherever they are in the world. Lastly, it is for all lovers of food, who can discover and create, what according to me, is the best cuisine in the world. Most importantly, this book is an ode to all grandmothers who carry with them the treasures of our history, of who we are and the foods that define us.

From left to right: Raan, Shammi Kebabs and Murgh Mussallam in process, often cooked outdoors.

SPICES & BASIC RECIPES

GARAM MASALA

INGREDIENTS

2½ Tbsp coriander seeds (*sabut dhaniya*)

2 Tbsp cumin seeds (*jeera sabut*)

2 Tbsp black peppercorns (*kali mirch sabut*)

10-12 cloves (*laung*)

1½ Tbsp green cardamom (*hari elaichi*) pods

2-3 black cardamom (*kali elaichi*) pods

3-4 mace (*javitri*)

7-8 bay leaves (*tej patta*)

¼ Tbsp nutmeg (*jaiphal*)

1 cinnamon (*dal chini*) stick

METHOD

1. Heat a heavy-base pan for 2 to 3 minutes over high heat. Reduce the heat to low, and add all the ingredients to the pan. Lightly toast them for 2 minutes, until aromatic.
2. Remove from heat and let the ingredients cool for 2 minutes.
3. Add them to a spice grinder jar and grind at medium setting to make a fine powder.
4. Sieve the mix after blending. Store the garam masala in an airtight container.

PREPARATION TIME: **3-5 MINUTES**

MAKES: **75 G**

CHAAT MASALA

INGREDIENTS

¼ cup cumin seeds (*jeera sabut*)

2 Tbsp coriander seeds (*sabut dhaniya*)

1 (2") piece dried ginger (*sonth*)

1 dried red chilli (*sabut sookhi lal mirch*)

2 Tbsp black pepper (*kali mirch*) powder

½ tsp cloves (*laung*)

½ Tbsp nutmeg (*jaiphal*) powder

3 Tbsp mint leaves (*pudina*)

¼ cup mango powder (*amchoor*)

Pinch of asafoetida (*hing*)

1 tsp salt

METHOD

1. In a heavy-bottomed pan over high heat, add the cumin and coriander seeds and dry roast for 2-3 minutes until the spices turn aromatic. Remove from heat, transfer to a plate and set aside to cool.
2. In the same pan over medium heat, add the dried ginger, dried red chilli, black pepper powder, cloves, and nutmeg and dry roast them for 2-3 minutes until aromatic. Remove from heat and let the spices to cool completely. Once cool, add the mint leaves and roast over low heat with the other ingredients for 2 minutes until the mint leaves are crisp.
3. Transfer to the same plate and let all the ingredients cool.
4. Add the dry mango powder, asafoetida, and salt to the ingredients in the plate.
5. Transfer the ingredients to a spice grinder and grind for 2-3 minutes to a fine powder on a low setting. Store the masala in an airtight jar.

PREPARATION TIME: **30 MINUTES**

MAKES: **100 G**

BIRYANI MASALA

INGREDIENTS

3-4 dried Kashmiri red chillies (*Kashmiri sookhi lal mirch*)

7-8 bay leaves (*tej patta*)

2 Tbsp coriander seeds (*sabut dhaniya*)

1 Tbsp cumin seeds (*jeera sabut*)

1 Tbsp caraway seeds (*shahi jeera*)

3 maces (*javitri*)

1 cinnamon (*dal chini*) stick

1 nutmeg (*jaiphal*)

1 tsp cloves (*laung*)

3 black cardamom (*badi elaichi*) pods

3 star anise (*chakri ke phool*)

10-12 green cardamom (*hari elaichi*) pods

1 Tbsp black peppercorns (*kali mirch*)

1 tsp fennel seeds (*saunf*)

½ tsp turmeric (*haldi*) powder

PREPARATION TIME: **15 MINUTES**

METHOD

1. In a heavy-bottomed pan over high heat, dry roast the red chillies and bay leaves for 2-3 minutes until they turn crisp. Remove from heat, transfer to a plate and set aside to cool for 2-3 minutes.
2. In the same pan over medium heat, dry roast the coriander seeds, cumin and caraway seeds until they turn aromatic. Remove from heat and transfer to the same plate as the chilli and bay leaves and set aside.
3. In the same pan over medium heat, dry roast the mace, cinnamon, nutmeg, cloves, black cardamom, star anise, green cardamom, black peppercorns, and fennel seeds. Remove from heat and let the ingredients cool for 2 minutes.
4. Now add the turmeric powder and combine well. Transfer the ingredients to a mixer-grinder. Grind the ingredients at a low setting for 2 minutes until finely powdered. Store the powder in an airtight container.

MAKES: **65 G**

NIHARI MIXED MASALA

INGREDIENTS

WHOLE SPICES:

2 Tbsp coriander seeds (*sabut dhaniya*)

1 Tbsp fennel seeds (*saunf*)

½ Tbsp black peppercorns (*kali mirch sabut*)

10-12 green cardamom (*hari elaichi*) pods

10 cloves (*laung*)

1-2 black cardamom (*kali elaichi*) pods

8-10 bay leaves (*tej patta*)

1 cinnamon (*dal chini*) stick

2 star anise (*chakri ke phool*)

½ Tbsp cumin seeds (*jeera sabut*)

¼ nutmeg (*jaiphal*)

4-5 g mace (*javitri*)

2 long peppers (*lambi kali mirch*)

10 g dried ginger (*sonth*)

1-2 dried red chilli (*lal sabut sookhi mirch*)

1 tsp dry papaya powder (available at grocery stores)

½ tsp carom seeds (*ajwain*)

½ Tbsp caraway seeds (*shahi jeera*)

½ Tbsp nigella seeds (*kalonji*)

SPICE POWDERS:

1 Tbsp coriander (*dhaniya*) powder

1 Tbsp Kashmiri red chilli (*lal mirch*) powder

¼ tsp turmeric (*haldi*) powder

METHOD

1. Combine all the whole spices in a jar of the mixer-grinder and grind at a low setting until finely powdered. Transfer to a mixing bowl.
2. Now add the coriander, red chilli and turmeric powders to the ground whole spices in the bowl and combine well. Store in an airtight container.

PREPARATION TIME: **10 MINUTES**

MAKES: **90 G**

HALEEM MASALA

INGREDIENTS

WHOLE SPICES:

1 Tbsp coriander seeds (*sabut dhaniya*)

2 Tbsp cumin seeds (*jeera sabut*)

1 tsp carom seeds (*ajwain*)

1 Tbsp caraway seeds (*shahi jeera*)

2-3 bay leaves (*tej patta*)

1 cinnamon (*dal chini*) stick

2-3 black cardamom (*kali elaichi*) pods

4-5 green cardamom (*hari elaichi*) pods

3-4 cloves (*laung*)

2 Tbsp fennel seeds (*saunf*)

10-15 red button chillies or dried red chillies (*sabut lal mirch*)

½ Tbsp black peppercorns (*kali mirch sabut*)

OTHER INGREDIENTS:

1½ tsp turmeric (*haldi*) powder

½ tsp salt

PREPARATION TIME: **15 MINUTES**

METHOD

1. In a pan over low heat, add all the whole spices and dry roast them for a minute until fragrant.
2. Add the turmeric powder and salt to the pan and after a minute transfer all the ingredients to a mortar. Hand-grind with a pestle until finely powdered.
3. Sieve the powder and discard the rest. Store in a glass container.

MAKES: **90 G**

GINGER-GARLIC PASTE

INGREDIENTS

50 g ginger

50 g garlic

PREPARATION TIME: **15-20 MINUTES**

METHOD

1. Peel and chop equal portions of ginger and garlic and add them to a blender jar.
2. Blend at medium-high setting for 2 to 3 minutes to make a smooth paste.
3. Store the paste in an air-tight glass jar. The paste can be refrigerated and stored for up to 7 days.

MAKES: **75 G**

TOMATO PASTE

INGREDIENTS

1 kg tomatoes, chopped

PREPARATION TIME: **5 MINUTES**

METHOD

1. Blend the tomatoes in a mixer jar at a medium-high setting for 2 to 3 minutes to make a smooth paste.
2. Remove from the mixer and store in a jar. The paste can be refrigerated and used for up to 7 days.

MAKES: **1 KG**

ONION PASTE

INGREDIENTS

500 g onions, chopped

½ cup water

PREPARATION TIME: **5 MINUTES**

METHOD

1. Blend the onions and water in a mixer jar at medium setting for 2 to 3 minutes to make a smooth paste.
2. Remove from the mixer and store in a jar. The paste can be refrigerated and stored for up to 2-3 days.

MAKES: **500 G**

TOMATO PUREE

INGREDIENTS

½ ltr water

½ kg tomatoes

PREPARATION TIME: **30 MINUTES**

METHOD

1. In a cooking pot over high heat, heat the water. Add the tomatoes and boil them for 15 to 20 minutes.
2. Remove from the heat and allow the tomatoes to cool before peeling them.
3. Blend the peeled tomatoes in a mixer jar at medium-high setting for 2 to 3 minutes to make a smooth paste. Add ½ cup water, if required to achieve the desired consistency.
4. Remove from the mixer and store in a jar. The puree can be refrigerated and stored for up to 7 days.

MAKES: **400 G**

TAMARIND PASTE

INGREDIENTS

250 g tamarind (*imli*)

3 cups water

METHOD

1. Rinse the tamarind thoroughly and remove the seeds.
2. In a pan over medium heat, heat 2 cups water. Remove the pan from heat and soak the tamarind in this water for 1 hour.
3. Drain excess water and transfer the soaked tamarind into a blender and blend at medium setting for 2 to 3 minutes until smooth.
4. Mash it with a ladle and add the remaining 1 cup of water.
5. Filter the tamarind pulp through a sieve into another pan.
6. Now place the pan over medium heat and cover with a lid. Cook for 5 minutes, stirring occasionally.
7. Remove from heat and store in a glass jar. It can be refrigerated and stored for 10-12 days.

PREPARATION TIME: **30 MINUTES**

MAKES: **250 G**

GREEN CHUTNEY

INGREDIENTS

30 g fresh coriander (*dhaniya*), chopped

30 g mint (*pudina*) leaves, chopped (optional)*

10-12 green chillies (*hari mirch*)

6-7 garlic cloves, roasted

1 tsp cumin (*jeera*) powder

2 lemons, juiced

METHOD

1. Add all the ingredients to a mixer blender jar. Blend at medium setting for 2 to 3 minutes to make a smooth paste.
2. Store in an airtight jar. The chutney can be refrigerated and stored for up to 7-8 days.

* Mint leaves can be added to the same recipe to make a mint chutney.

PREPARATION TIME: **10 MINUTES**

MAKES: **75 G**

SNACKS

KATHAL KEBAB

Tender and flavourful jackfruit kebabs

INGREDIENTS

1 kg diced jackfruit (*kathal*)

1½ cups Bengal gram (chana dal), boiled

1 tsp red chilli (*kutti lal mirch*) powder

1 tsp garam masala (p. 16)

1 medium onion, sliced

1 Maggi Magic Vegetarian Cube

1 Tbsp ginger-garlic paste (p. 21)

1 tsp salt

1 medium onion, finely chopped

5-6 green chillies (*hari mirch*), chopped

2-3 Tbsp fresh coriander (*dhaniya*), chopped

1 Tbsp gram flour (*besan*), roasted

1 cup refined oil

METHOD

1. In a pressure cooker over high heat, combine the jackfruit, chana dal, chilli powder, garam masala, onion, Maggi cube, ginger-garlic paste, and salt with 2 cups of water.
2. Lock the lid in place and cook for 20 to 25 minutes, or until 3-4 whistles are released, ensuring that the dal and jackfruit are thoroughly cooked. Remove from heat.
3. Let the pressure release and open the lid. Allow the mixture to cool and transfer it to a blender. Grind it over medium setting until it turns into a thick paste.
4. Add the finely chopped onions, green chilli, and coriander to the paste and mix well. Stir in the roasted besan and gently knead the mixture.
5. Wet your hands and taking small portions shape the mixture into equal-sized round, flat kebabs of 2 to 3 inch diametre.
6. In a large heavy-bottomed frying pan, add 3 Tbsp oil (for a batch of 4-5 kebabs). Shallow fry the kebabs in small batches until golden brown on both sides.
7. Serve hot with sliced onions and green chutney (p. 23).

COOKING TIME: **60 MINUTES**

MAKES: **20-22**

VEG SEEKH KEBAB

Vegetables and cheese minced kebabs

INGREDIENTS

4-5 (200 g) potatoes

2 Tbsp refined oil

300 g french beans, finely chopped

4-5 (250 g) carrots, finely chopped

250 g paneer, grated

2 cheese cubes, grated

1 (1") piece ginger, chopped

½ cup fresh coriander (*dhaniya*)

2 green chillies (*hari mirch*), chopped

4 tsp gram flour (*besan*)

SPICES:

1 tsp coriander (*dhaniya*) powder

1 tsp Kitchen King masala

1 tsp salt

1 tsp turmeric (*haldi*) powder

1 tsp chaat masala (p. 17)

1 tsp garam masala (p. 16)

½ tsp dry mango (*aamchoor*) powder

METHOD

1. In a cooking pot over high heat, add the potatoes with ½ litre water (enough to submerge the potatoes) and bring to a boil. Simmer for about 15 to 20 minutes or until the potatoes are tender. You can pierce with a fork to ensure they are done. Peel and mash them using a potato masher or fork. Set aside.
2. In a fry pan over medium heat, add the oil and sauté the french beans and carrots until they soften. Allow them to cool and set aside.
3. In a large bowl, combine the mashed potatoes, sautéed carrots and beans, grated paneer, cheese, ginger, coriander leaves, green chillies, and gram flour. Add the spices and knead the mixture into a dough.
4. Portion the dough into equal cylindrical kebabs.

TO COOK ON THE TANDOOR:

5. Thread the kebabs onto metal skewers (2-3 in one skewer) of 5 inches each, and grill them over a charcoal grill. Baste them with oil while grilling and cook evenly by rotating the skewers as needed until the kebabs are golden brown.

OR TO COOK ON THE STOVETOP:

6. In a small bowl, add ½ Tbsp ghee or butter. Burn a small piece of charcoal and place it in the centre on top of the ghee.
7. Create a well in the centre of the bowl and place the small bowl with coal in the centre of the larger bowl and cover for 3 minutes to smoke the kebabs.
8. Heat ½ tsp ghee (for one batch of 4 kebabs) in a grilling pan over medium heat.
9. Transfer the kebabs in batches onto the grilling pan and cook for about 2 to 3 minutes until golden brown; flipping them to cook all around. Remove from heat and repeat the process for the remaining kebabs.
10. Serve hot with green chutney (p. 23) and onions.

COOKING TIME: **40 MINUTES**

MAKES: **15-20**

BONE-IN CHICKEN TIKKA

Marinated chicken chunks, skewered and grilled to perfection

INGREDIENTS

1 kg bone-in chicken, skinless

FOR THE MARINADE:

3 Tbsp vinegar (preferably Heinz distilled malt)

1 tsp Kashmiri red chilli (*mirch*) powder

1 tsp red chilli pepper (*degi mirch*) powder

Salt, to taste

1 tsp lemon juice

1 Tbsp ginger-garlic paste (p. 21)

Refined oil, for basting

METHOD

1. Halve the chicken into two pieces.
2. In a large bowl combine the vinegar, red chilli powder, red chilli pepper, lemon juice, ginger-garlic paste and season to taste with salt.
3. Rub the marinade all over the chicken and in the same bowl refrigerate overnight. You can cover the bowl with a flat plate or with a foil.

TO BARBEQUE ON THE TANDOOR:

4. Take the bowl out atleast an hour before you cook. Thread the meat onto metal skewers and grill them over a charcoal grill (tandoor). Baste frequently with oil while grilling and cook evenly by rotating the skewers as needed until the meat turns golden brown.

OR TO COOK ON THE STOVETOP:

5. In a bowl, add the marinated meat and create a well in the centre.
6. In a small bowl, add ½ Tbsp ghee or butter. Burn a small piece of charcoal and place it in the bowl with the butter. Place this bowl in the centre of the larger bowl with the marinated meat and cover for 3 minutes to smoke the meat.
7. Thread the smoked meat onto skewers.
8. Heat ½ tsp ghee (for 4 kebabs) in a grilling pan over high heat for 2 to 3 minutes. Remove the skewered chunks and transfer onto the grilling pan. Cook for 8-10 minutes until the meat turns golden brown and then flip the meat to ensure both sides are cooked. Repeat the process for the remaining pieces.
9. Remove from heat and serve with green chutney (p. 23).

COOKING TIME: **2½ HOURS**

MAKES: **8-10**

CHICKEN SEEKH KEBAB

Melt-in-your-mouth chicken kebabs

INGREDIENTS

1 kg minced chicken (*keema*), (machine-minced)

3 small onions, fried, dried and ground

1 large onion, chopped

2 Tbsp gram flour (*besan*), roasted

½ tsp garam masala (p. 16)

1 tsp wild melon (*kachri*) powder

1 tsp yellow chilli (*peeli mirch*) powder

Salt, to taste

1 Tbsp ginger-garlic paste (p. 21)

150-200 g seekh kebab masala (store bought)

50 g fresh coriander (*dhaniya*), chopped

5-6 green chillies (*hari mirch*), chopped

½ Tbsp oil, to baste/grill

½ cup ghee

METHOD

1. In a large bowl, add the chicken keema, ground onions, chopped onion, besan, garam masala, wild melon powder, and yellow chilli powder. Season to taste with salt.
2. Add the ginger-garlic paste, seekh kebab masala, coriander, and green chillies. Combine well and set aside to marinate for 1 hour.

TO COOK ON THE TANDOOR:

3. Thread the meat onto metal skewers and grill them over a charcoal grill (tandoor). Baste frequently with oil while grilling and cook evenly by rotating the skewers as needed until the meat turns golden brown.

OR TO COOK ON THE STOVETOP:

4. In a bowl, add the marinated meat and create a well in the centre.
5. In a small bowl, add ½ Tbsp ghee or butter. Burn a small piece of charcoal and place it in the small bowl with the butter. Place the small bowl in the centre of the larger bowl with the marinated meat and cover fully for 3 minutes to smoke the meat.
6. Carefully mould the smoked meat onto the skewers, making sure it is pressed firmly, approximately 5 inches in length.
7. Heat ½ tsp ghee (for 4 kebabs) in a grilling pan over high heat for 2-3 minutes. Remove the skewered chunks and transfer onto the grilling pan. Cook for 8-10 minutes until the meat turns golden brown, flipping them to brown all around. Repeat the process for the remaining kebabs.
8. Remove from heat and serve with roomali rotis (p. 157), green chutney (p. 23), and onion rings.

COOKING TIME: **60 MINUTES**

MAKES: **20-22**

MUTTON KACCHI TIKKI

Minced lamb patties marinated with spices

INGREDIENTS

4 slices of bread

45 ml refined oil

1 kg minced mutton/lamb (*keema*)

4 onions (2 chopped + 2 finely sliced)

3 Tbsp gram flour (*besan*), roasted

2 eggs, beaten

4-5 green chillies (*hari mirch*), chopped

50 g fresh coriander (*dhaniya*), chopped

1 tsp garam masala (p. 16)

1 tsp chaat masala (p. 17)

1 tsp salt

1 Tbsp ginger-garlic paste (p. 21)

METHOD

1. Soak the bread slices in 50 ml water for 10 seconds. Squeeze out the water and crumble. Set the breadcrumbs aside.
2. In a small wok over medium heat, add 1 Tbsp oil and fry the sliced onions until brown. Remove from heat, transfer to a small bowl and set aside.
3. In a large bowl, marinate the minced meat with chopped onions, gram flour, eggs, breadcrumbs, fried onions, green chilli, fresh coriander, garam masala, chaat masala, salt, and ginger-garlic paste. Combine well using your hands and set aside for 30 minutes. Divide into roundels of preferred sizes and flatten the roundels.
4. In a pan over medium-to-slow heat, add 2 Tbsp oil (for every 4-5 tikkis). Place the flattened tikkis on the pan and shallow fry each side of the tikki for 2-3 minutes until it turns golden brown. Repeat with the remaining tikkis. Serve hot with green chutney (p. 23) and onion rings.

COOKING TIME: **50 MINUTES**

MAKES: **20-22 TIKKIS**

LAHORI SEEKH KEBAB

Spicy minced mutton kebabs

INGREDIENTS

1 kg minced mutton/lamb (*keema*)

200 g lamb fat (*charbi*)

8 large onions, made to a paste (p. 22)

2 Tbsp Madras curry powder (preferably Green Label)

1 tsp black pepper (*kali mirch*) powder

1 tsp turmeric (*haldi*) powder

1 Tbsp bicarb soda (*meetha* soda)

2 tsp sumac

Salt, to taste

½ Tbsp oil, to baste/grill

METHOD

1. In a large bowl, combine the minced meat with lamb fat.
2. Place the onion paste in a muslin bag and squeeze to drain the water. Set the pulp extract aside.
3. Add the onion paste extract, Madras curry powder, black pepper powder, turmeric, and bicarb soda to the meat. Season to taste with salt and combine well. Cover the bowl and refrigerate for 30 minutes.

TO COOK ON THE TANDOOR:

4. Thread the meat onto metal skewers and grill them over a charcoal grill (tandoor). Baste frequently with oil while grilling and cook evenly by rotating the skewers as needed until the meat turns golden brown.

OR TO COOK ON THE STOVETOP:

5. Create a well in the centre of the bowl with marinated meat.
6. In a small bowl, add ½ Tbsp ghee or butter. Burn a small piece of charcoal and place it in the small bowl. Place the small bowl in the centre of the larger bowl with the marinated meat and cover for 3 minutes to smoke the meat.
7. Thread the smoked meat onto skewers.
8. Heat ½ tsp ghee (for 4 kebabs) in a grilling pan over high heat for 2-3 minutes. Remove the skewered chunks and transfer onto the grilling pan. Cook for 10-12 minutes until the meat turns golden brown, flipping to ensure all sides are cooked. Repeat the process for the remaining kebabs.
9. When done, sprinkle sumac on a platter, place the kebabs on it and serve hot with Sesame Naan (p. 155) or rice.

COOKING TIME: **60 MINUTES**

MAKES: **16-18**

MUTTON CHOP FRY

Deep-fried marinated mutton patties

INGREDIENTS

1 kg mutton/lamb chops

2 eggs, beaten

1 Tbsp corn flour

1 tsp white pepper (*safed mirch*) powder

1 tsp black pepper (*kali mirch*) crushed

Salt, to taste

1 Tbsp ginger-garlic paste (p. 31)

½ lemon, juiced

500 ml refined oil

Chaat masala, to taste (p. 17)

METHOD

1. With a heavy, flat object, such as a skillet or a meat mallet, pound the meat to flatten it.
2. In a large bowl, add the beaten eggs, corn flour, white pepper, black pepper, salt, ginger-garlic paste, and lemon juice. Add the meat chops and combine well. Set aside for half an hour.
3. In a wok over high heat, add the oil and let it sizzle. Reduce the heat to medium.
4. Deep fry the marinated chops for 3-5 minutes in small batches until they turn golden brown. Repeat the process with the remaining chops.
5. Use a slotted spoon and drain the chops of excess oil on absorbent paper or kitchen towels. Serve with a sprinkle of chaat masala and mint chutney (p. 23).

COOKING TIME: **60 MINUTES**

MAKES: **6-8**

MUTTON CHOPS WITH ONION

Spiced meat chops balanced with yoghurt

INGREDIENTS

1 kg mutton/lamb chops

3 Tbsp ginger-garlic paste (p. 21)

1 Tbsp salt, or to taste

100 ml refined oil

½ tsp cumin seeds (*jeera sabut*)

2 medium onions, sliced

6 dry red chilli peppers (*lal mirch*)

Small piece ginger, julienned

4 garlic cloves, sliced

WHOLE SPICES:

1 small cinnamon (*dal chini*) stick

1-2 bay leaves (*tej patta*)

4-5 cloves (*laung*)

3 Tbsp yoghurt (*dahi*)

1 Tbsp garam masala (p. 16)

1 lemon, juiced

½ Tbsp chaat masala (p. 17)

6-8 green chillies (*hari mirch*), chopped

METHOD

1. Place a pressure cooker over high heat for 2 to 3 minutes. Add the meat chops, ginger-garlic paste, salt, and ½ cup water. Lock the lid in place and pressure cook for 10 minutes, or until 2-3 whistles. Turn off the heat.
2. Let the pressure release. Open the lid and return the cooker over medium heat. Continue cooking for 5-7 minutes or until the excess water evaporates.
3. In a wok over high heat, add the oil and heat it for 2-3 minutes. Reduce the heat to medium. Add the cumin seeds and onions, and sauté until the onions turn pink. Add the dry red chilli peppers, ginger, garlic and stir well.
4. In a small muslin bag for spices, add the cinnamon stick, bay leaves and cloves, and drop it into the wok. Now stir in the yoghurt and continue cooking, stirring frequently.
5. Add the garam masala, lemon juice, chaat masala, and green chillies. Reduce the heat to low and cover the wok with a lid. Cook for 10-15 minutes, stirring occasionally.
6. Once the meat is cooked and turns light brown, remove from heat. Discard the spice bag and serve hot.

COOKING TIME: **60 MINUTES**

SERVES: **4-6**

MUTTON SEEKH KEBAB

Melt-in-your-mouth mutton kebabs

INGREDIENTS

1 large onion, chopped

500 g minced mutton/lamb (*keema*), coarsely minced

150 g mutton fat (*charbi*)

½ Tbsp oil, to baste/grill

FOR THE MARINADE:

1 tsp chilli flakes

¾ tsp fresh coriander (*dhaniya*), crushed

¾ tsp red chilli powder (*lal mirch*)

½ Tbsp wild melon (*kachri*) powder

2 pinches of bi-carb soda

Salt, to taste

METHOD

1. Refrigerate the chopped onion in a bowl for 4 hours or overnight to drain its water.
2. In a large bowl, add the minced meat and fat. Add the chilli flakes, coriander, red chilli powder, wild melon powder, bi-carb soda and salt, and marinate for 4 hours.

TO COOK ON THE TANDOOR:

3. Thread the meat onto metal skewers and grill them over a charcoal grill (tandoor). Baste frequently with oil while grilling and cook evenly by rotating the skewers as needed till the meat turns golden brown.

OR TO COOK ON THE STOVETOP:

4. In a large bowl, add the marinated meat and create a well in the centre.
5. In a small bowl, add ½ Tbsp ghee or butter. Burn a small piece of charcoal and place it in the small bowl with the butter. Place the small bowl in the centre of the larger bowl with the marinated meat and cover for 3 minutes to smoke the meat.
6. Thread the smoked meat onto skewers.
7. Heat ½ tsp ghee (for 4 kebabs) in a grilling pan over medium heat for 2-3 minutes. Remove the skewered chunks and transfer onto the grilling pan. Cook for 10-12 minutes until the meat turns golden brown and all sides are cooked. Repeat for the remaining kebabs.
8. Remove from heat and serve with roomali rotis (p. 157) and green chutney (p. 23).

COOKING TIME: **30 MINUTES**

MAKES: **10-12 KEBABS**

MUTTON ALOO CHOP FRY

Mutton chops coated with potato crumbs and fried

INGREDIENTS

90 ml refined oil

1 kg mutton/lamb chops

2 Tbsp ginger-garlic paste (p. 21)

1 cup water

Salt, to taste

50 g fresh coriander (*dhaniya*), chopped

6 green chillies (*hari mirch*), chopped

1 tsp chaat masala (p. 17)

1 lemon, juiced

2 Tbsp breadcrumbs

8 medium-sized potatoes, boiled and mashed

2 eggs, beaten

1½ cup oil, for deep frying

METHOD

1. In a pressure cooker over low heat, add the oil. Once the oil begins to sizzle, add the meat chops, ginger-garlic paste, 1 cup water, and season to taste with salt. Close the lid and cook for 10 minutes, or until 2 whistles. Remove from heat and let the pressure release.
2. Open the lid of the pressure cooker and continue cooking the chops over high heat until the water evaporates completely. Remove from the heat.
3. Pound the chops with a meat pounder and then flatten by pressing your palm on it. Set aside for 30 minutes.
4. In a large bowl, add the coriander leaves, green chillies, chaat masala, lemon juice, 1 Tbsp breadcrumbs and combine with mashed potatoes. Cover the chops with this mixture.
5. In a separate bowl, add the beaten eggs and dip each chop separately in them. Coat them with the remaining breadcrumbs.
6. Heat the oil in a wok over medium heat and in batches, deep fry the chops until they turn golden. Use a slotted spoon and drain on kitchen towels. Serve with green chutney (p. 23).

COOKING TIME: **45 MINUTES**

MAKES: **6-8**

NAMKEEN GOSHT

Grilled chunks of tender meat

INGREDIENTS

1 kg neck pieces of mutton

150 g mutton/lamb fat (*charbi*)

½ Tbsp Ajinomoto (optional)

3 tsp black peppercorns (*kali mirch*), crushed

2 tsp salt, or to taste

METHOD

1. In a large bowl, combine the mutton pieces and fat together with Ajinomoto (if using), and black peppercorns. Season to taste with salt. Allow it to marinate overnight or for 8 hours in the refrigerator.
2. In a pressure cooker over high heat, add the marinated meat and 2 Tbsp of water and close the lid. Pressure cook for 10 minutes, for 3-4 whistles.
3. Remove from heat and let the pressure release. Open the lid and return the cooker over medium heat. Simmer until any excess water evaporates and the meat is tender.
4. Preheat the oven or grill to 150°C.
5. Transfer the cooked meat pieces on a foilsheet, ensuring that they are completely covered from all sides.
6. Transfer the foil-covered meat into the oven or grill and cook for 25-30 minutes, or until golden brown.
7. Remove from the oven or grill and serve immediately.

COOKING TIME: **60 MINUTES**

SERVES: **6-8**

CHAPLI KEBAB

Traditional spiced minced mutton and egg kebabs

INGREDIENTS

1 kg minced mutton/lamb (*keema*)

200 g mutton fat (*charbi*)

2-3 medium-sized onions, chopped

1 Tbsp ginger-garlic paste (p. 21)

1 Tbsp chopped fresh coriander (*dhaniya*)

2-3 green chillies (*hari mirch*), chopped

5 medium-sized tomatoes, chopped and hand-squeezed to drain their juice

4 Tbsp gram flour (*besan*)

100 g chapli kebab masala (store bought)

6 eggs, scrambled

4 Tbsp corn flour

3 eggs

4 Tbsp refined oil, to shallow fry

METHOD

1. In a large bowl, combine the minced mutton, mutton fat, onions, ginger-garlic paste, coriander, green chillies, tomatoes, gram flour, chapli kabab masala, scrambled eggs, and corn flour. Crack 3 eggs into the mixture and combine well. Knead the kebab mixture into a soft dough and refrigerate for 1 hour. You can cover the bowl with a flat plate or foil.
2. Wet your hands and portion the dough into equal-sized, large, flat roundels.
3. In a heavy-based fry pan over high heat, add the oil. Once the oil is smoky, reduce the heat to medium-low. In small batches, shallow-fry the kebabs for about 4-6 minutes on each side or until both sides are charred and the edges are crisp. Repeat for the remaining kebabs.
4. Serve hot with tandoori rotis (p. 156), onions, and green chutney (p. 23).

COOKING TIME: **60 MINUTES**

MAKES: **20-22**

SHAMMI KEBAB

Minced lamb kebabs

INGREDIENTS

WHOLE SPICES:

2 bay leaves (*tej patta*)

4 cloves (*laung*)

4 green cardamom (*hari elaichi*) pods

2 cinnamon (*dal chini*) sticks

2 Tbsp black pepper corns (*kali mirch*)

1 star anise (*chakri ke phool*)

2 black cardamom (*moti elaichi*) pods

1 tsp cumin seeds (*jeera*)

OTHER INGREDIENTS:

1 kg minced mutton/lamb (*keema*), hand ground

400 g Bengal gram (*chana dal*), rinsed

1 onion, chopped

Salt, to taste

3-4 green chillies (*hari mirch*), chopped

50 g fresh coriander (*dhaniya*), chopped

1 onion, sliced and fried until brown

1 tsp chaat masala (p. 17)

1 tsp garam masala (p. 16)

2 eggs, beaten

120 ml refined oil

METHOD

1. In a muslin spice bag, add all the whole spices and set aside.
2. In a pressure cooker over high heat, add the minced meat, chana dal, onion, and the muslin bag of whole spices. Season to taste with salt. Close the lid and cook for one whistle. Remove from heat and let the pressure release.
3. Open the lid of the cooker and place it over low heat. Simmer for 25 minutes. Remove from heat and set aside to cool.
4. Remove the muslin bag of whole spices and transfer the minced meat mixture to a mixer-grinder. Grind at medium setting until the meat is properly minced into a thick paste. Transfer the minced meat into a bowl.
5. Add the green chillies, fresh coriander, brown onion, chaat masala, garam masala, and beaten eggs.
6. Knead the mixture into a dough. Divide the dough into roundels of preferred sizes and flatten them by hand.
7. Heat the oil in a frying pan over low heat. Shallow fry each side for 2 to 3 minutes until golden brown. Use a slotted spoon and drain on kitchen towels. Repeat with the remaining roundels.
8. Serve hot with green chutney (p. 23) and onion rings.

COOKING TIME: **60 MINUTES**

MAKES: **20-22 PIECES**

FRIED FISH WITH MASALA

Rampuri-style spicy fish tikka

INGREDIENTS

1 kg sole fish, chopped

½ Tbsp turmeric (*haldi*) powder

1 Tbsp ginger-garlic paste (p. 21)

1½ Tbsp lemon juice

Salt, to taste

150 ml mustard oil

1 tsp cumin seeds (*jeera*)

2 onions, chopped

2 tomatoes, chopped

½ Tbsp garam masala (p. 16)

½ Tbsp chilli pepper (*degi mirch*) powder

1 tsp coriander (*dhaniya*) powder

1 tsp black mustard seeds (*kali sarson*)

1 tsp red mustard seeds (*lal sarso*)

1 tsp black peppercorns (*kali mirch*), crushed

1 tsp water

2-3 green chillies (*hari mirch*), slit

30 g fresh coriander (*dhaniya*), chopped

½ Tbsp chaat masala (p. 17)

METHOD

1. Rinse the fish under running water thoroughly.
2. In a large bowl, combine the turmeric and ½ tsp ginger-garlic paste. Rub this mixture all over the fish and set aside for 10 minutes. Apply lemon juice over the fish until there is no fishy smell remaining. Dry it over a muslin cloth and transfer into a large bowl.
3. Season to taste with salt.
4. In a heavy-bottomed broad pan over high heat, add 6 Tbsp mustard oil and wait until it simmers. Reduce the heat to medium, and in batches, shallow fry the fish until golden brown on both sides. Set aside.

TO MAKE THE MASALA:

5. In a pan over high heat, add 4 Tbsp mustard oil and wait until it bubbles. Add the cumin seeds and reduce the heat to medium-low. Once the cumin seeds splutter, add the onions and sauté until they turn pink.
6. Now add the tomatoes, the remaining ginger-garlic paste, garam masala, chilli pepper powder, coriander powder, black mustard, red mustard, and crushed black pepper. Simmer for 15-20 minutes.
7. Reduce the heat and add the shallow-fried fish. Simmer for 5-10 minutes. Cover the pan with a lid and cook for 2-3 minutes. Remove from the heat.
8. Garnish with slit green chillies, coriander, and chaat masala. Serve hot.

COOKING TIME: **60 MINUTES**

SERVES: **5-6**

FISH FRY

Shallow-fried fish, spiced to perfection

INGREDIENTS

1 ltr water

2 lemons, juiced (1 for soaking + 1 for garnishing)

1 Tbsp ginger-garlic paste (p. 21)

1 kg sole fish, chopped

1 cup gram flour (*besan*)

1 Tbsp chilli pepper (*degi mirch*) powder

1 Tbsp coriander (*dhaniya*) powder

½ Tbsp turmeric (*haldi*) powder

2-3 green chillies (*hari mirch*)

Salt, to taste

50 g fresh coriander (*dhaniya*), chopped

250 ml refined oil

1 Tbsp chaat masala (p. 17)

METHOD

1. In a large bowl, add 1 litre water, juice of 1 lemon and ginger-garlic paste. Soak the fish in the prepared water for 15 minutes. Rinse it thoroughly until there is no smell. Dry it over a muslin cloth, and transfer into a separate large bowl.
2. In another bowl, combine the gram flour, chilli pepper powder, coriander powder, turmeric, green chillies, salt, and coriander leaves. Add 2 to 3 Tbsp of water to make a paste and rub all over the fish to marinate for half an hour.
3. In a heavy-bottomed broad pan over low heat, add the oil and let it simmer. Shallow fry the marinated fish, one/two pieces at a time.
4. Use a slotted spoon and drain on absorbent paper or kitchen towels to remove excess oil. Garnish with the remaining lemon juice and chaat masala and serve hot with green chutney (p. 23).

COOKING TIME: **45 MINUTES**

SERVES: **4-5**

MAINS
VEGETARIAN

SAIM ALOO

Dry dish of flat beans and potatoes

INGREDIENTS

30 ml mustard oil

1 tsp cumin seeds (*jeera sabut*)

Pinch of asafoetida (*hing*)

8 garlic cloves, finely chopped

3-4 dry red chilli (*sookhi lal mirch*)

500 g flat beans (*saim*), rinsed and chopped

2 medium-sized potatoes, cubed into 8 pieces each

Salt, to taste

METHOD

1. Heat the oil in a wok over high heat for 2-3 minutes.
2. Reduce the heat to medium and add cumin seeds, asafoetida, garlic, dry red chilli and sauté for 2-3 minutes until the garlic becomes fragrant.
3. Add the flat beans and potatoes. Season to taste with salt. Cover the wok with a lid and cook for 15-20 minutes, stirring occasionally.
4. Cook until the preparation is dry and the oil separates. Serve hot with chappatis (p. 154).

COOKING TIME: **40 MINUTES**

SERVES: **2-3**

ARBI MASALA

Spicy taro root curry

INGREDIENTS

30 ml mustard oil

1 Tbsp cumin seeds (*jeera sabut*)

2 medium-sized onions, chopped

2 medium-sized tomatoes, chopped

1 Tbsp ginger-garlic paste (p. 21)

500 g taro root (*arbi*), peeled and each cubed into 8 pieces

1 tsp garam masala (p. 16)

1 tsp coriander (*dhaniya*) powder

1 tsp turmeric (*haldi*) powder

1 tsp red chilli (*lal mirch*) powder

Salt, to taste

Fresh coriander (*dhaniya*), chopped, to garnish

METHOD

1. Heat the oil in a wok over high heat for 2-3 minutes. Add the cumin seeds and let them splutter. Add the onions and sauté until light brown.
2. Reduce the heat to medium-low and add tomatoes and ginger-garlic paste. Sauté for 2 to 3 minutes, or until the tomatoes are tender.
3. Now add the taro root, garam masala, coriander powder, turmeric, and red chilli powder. Stir well.
4. Stir in 1 cup water and let simmer for 20-25 minutes over low heat, until the taro root softens and the water evaporates. Season to taste with salt and remove from heat.
5. Garnish with fresh coriander and serve hot with chappatis (p. 154).

COOKING TIME: **35-40 MINUTES**

SERVES: **4-5**

BHINDI

Stir-fried okra

INGREDIENTS

4 Tbsp mustard oil

3-4 dry red chilli (*sookhi lal mirch*)

1 Tbsp cumin seeds (*jeera sabut*)

2 medium-sized onions, sliced

1 kg okra (*bhindi*), rinsed, dried and chopped to small, round slices

1 tsp turmeric (*haldi*) powder

1 tsp coriander (*dhaniya*) powder

1 tsp red chilli (*lal mirch*) powder

Salt, to taste

METHOD

1. Heat the oil in a wok over high heat. Once the oil turns smoky, reduce the heat to medium. Add the dry red chillies and cumin seeds, and roast for 1 or 2 minutes.
2. Add the onions and sauté until brown.
3. Now add the okra, turmeric, coriander powder, red chilli powder, and season to taste with salt. Stir well.
4. Cover the wok with a lid and cook for 15 to 20 minutes. Stir occasionally and cook until the okra is cooked and no longer slimy. Remove from heat.
5. Serve hot with chappatis (p. 154).

COOKING TIME: **35-40 MINUTES**

SERVES: **4-6**

ARBI SOOKHI

Dry taro root, stir fried

INGREDIENTS

6Tbsp mustard oil

2 Tbsp carom seeds (*ajwain*)

6 garlic cloves, sliced

Pinch of asafoetida (*hing*)

1 kg fresh, seasonal taro root (*arbi*), rinsed, peeled, chopped to batons

2 Tbsp milk

Salt, to taste

6-8 green chillies (*hari mirch*), each slit in two halves

1 tsp turmeric (*haldi*) powder

1 tsp coriander (*dhaniya*) powder

1 tsp red chilli (*lal mirch*) powder

1 tsp cumin (*jeera*) powder

1 tsp chaat masala (p. 17)

METHOD

1. Heat the oil in a pressure cooker over high heat for 2 to 3 minutes. Add the carom seeds, garlic, and asafoetida; sauté for 2 minutes.
2. Add the taro root (arbi), milk, green chillies, and season to taste with salt. Close the lid of the pressure cooker and cook for 5 minutes, or until 2 whistles.
3. Let the pressure release and open the lid. Now add the turmeric, coriander powder, red chilli powder, and cumin powder.
4. Cook over high heat for 10-15 minutes, stirring continuously until the water evaporates.
5. Remove from heat, and sprinkle some chaat masala. Serve hot with chappatis (p. 154).

COOKING TIME: **25-30 MINUTES**

SERVES: **6-8**

ALOO TAMATAR

Flavourful curry of potatoes and tomatoes

INGREDIENTS

1 (2") piece ginger

10-12 garlic cloves

100 g ghee

250 g tomato puree (p. 22)

1 kg potatoes, boiled and cubed

1 tsp salt

Red chilli (*lal mirch*) powder, to taste

1 lemon, juiced

6 green chillies (*hari mirch*), slit lengthwise

METHOD

1. Grate the ginger and garlic and add to a muslin cloth to squeeze the juice out. Discard the pulp and set aside the juice.
2. In a large, heavy-based pan over high heat, add the ghee with garlic and ginger juice. Cook until aromatic.
3. Stir in the tomato puree and sauté until the ghee separates and rises to the surface.
4. Now add the potatoes, salt, and chilli powder. Reduce the heat and stir well.
5. Pour in one cup of water, and cover the pan with a lid. Cook for 5 minutes.
6. Remove the lid and add the lemon juice and green chillies. Mix well and simmer until the flavours meld. Remove from heat.
7. Serve hot with tandoori rotis (p. 156).

COOKING TIME: **40 MINUTES**

SERVES: **6-8**

ALOO BHARTA

Semi-dry preparation of roasted mashed potatoes

INGREDIENTS

2 Tbsp refined oil

1 Tbsp cumin seeds (*jeera sabut*)

4 dry red chillies (*sookhi lal mirch*)

1 medium-sized onion, finely chopped

1 kg potatoes, boiled and lightly mashed

Salt, to taste

1 tsp chaat masala (p. 17)

4-5 green chillies (*hari mirch*), chopped

½ lemon, juiced

50 g fresh coriander (*dhaniya*), chopped

METHOD

1. Heat the oil in a wok over high heat for 2 to 3 minutes. Add the cumin seeds and dry red chillies, and roast for 1 to 2 minutes.
2. Add the onion and sauté until light brown.
3. Now reduce the heat and add the mashed potatoes; season to taste with salt. Sprinkle the chaat masala, green chillies, and lemon juice. Stir well to combine.
4. Cover the wok with a lid and cook for 8-10 minutes, stirring occasionally.
5. Remove from heat and garnish with fresh coriander. Serve this semi-dry dish with chappatis (p. 154).

COOKING TIME: **40-45 MINUTES**

SERVES: **8-10**

BHINDI LAMBI

Dry dish of spiced okra

INGREDIENTS

2 Tbsp mustard oil

1 tsp cumin seeds (*jeera sabut*)

1 onion, chopped

1 tomato, chopped

1 Tbsp ginger-garlic paste (p. 21)

1 Tbsp turmeric (*haldi*) powder

½ Tbsp coriander (*dhaniya*) powder

½ Tbsp red chilli (*lal mirch*) powder

¼ Tbsp garam masala (p. 16)

1 Tbsp salt

½ kg okra (*bhindi*), rinsed, dried and slit lengthwise, with the tips cut off

METHOD

1. Heat the oil in a wok over high heat for 2 to 3 minutes. Reduce the heat to medium and add cumin seeds. Roast for 1 to 2 minutes.
2. Add the onions and sauté until soft.
3. Add the chopped tomatoes, ginger-garlic paste, turmeric, coriander powder, red chilli powder, and garam masala. Season to taste with salt.
4. Now add the okra and mix well.
5. Reduce the heat and cook for 15 to 20 minutes, or until the okra becomes tender and the preparation is dry. Stir the vegetable occasionally so that it does not stick to the base of the wok.
6. Remove from heat and serve hot with chappatis (p. 154).

COOKING TIME: **30 MINUTES**

SERVES: **4-5**

BANDH GOBHI

Stir fried cabbage

INGREDIENTS

20 ml mustard oil

1 tsp black mustard seeds (*kali sarson*)

1 Tbsp (2 stems) curry leaves (*kadipatta*)

3-4 green chillies (*hari mirch*), slit and halved

1 tsp turmeric (*haldi*) powder

Salt, to taste

½ kg cabbage (*bandh gobhi*), rinsed thoroughly and finely chopped

METHOD

1. Heat the oil in a wok over high heat until it becomes smoky. Reduce the heat to medium and add the black mustard seeds. Stir for 2 minutes until it starts to splutter.
2. Now add the curry leaves, green chillies, and turmeric. Season to taste with salt. Add the cabbage and mix well.
3. Reduce the heat and cook. Once the oil separates and the colour starts to change, increase the heat to high.
4. Cook for another 7 to 10 minutes until all the water dries out and the cabbage is tender and glossy.
5. Remove from heat and serve hot with chappatis (p. 154).

COOKING TIME: **33-35 MINUTES**

SERVES: **4-6**

CHAWLAI SAAG

Spicy dry dish of red amaranth

INGREDIENTS

1 kg red amaranth (*lal saag/ chawlai*)

30 ml mustard oil

1 Tbsp cumin seeds (*jeera sabut*)

Pinch of asafoetida (*hing*)

6 garlic cloves, chopped

6 dry red chillies (*sookhi lal mirch*)

½ tsp salt

METHOD

1. Rinse the red amaranth thoroughly in running water and then chop it.
2. Heat the oil in a wok over high heat for 2 to 3 minutes. Add the cumin seeds and roast for 1 to 2 minutes, or until they start to splutter.
3. Reduce the heat to medium and add asafoetida, garlic, red chillies, and chopped amaranth. Season to taste with salt. Mix well.
4. Cover the wok with a lid and cook for 15-20 minutes, stirring occasionally and checking the water. Cook until the preparation dries out and softens.
5. Serve hot with chappatis (p. 154) or enjoy with rice and dal.

COOKING TIME: **30-35 MINUTES**

SERVES: **4-5**

PANEER PASANDA

Rich dish of stuffed paneer with gravy

INGREDIENTS

500 g paneer, cut into large triangular pieces

FOR THE STUFFING:

4-5 cashews, chopped

1 tsp fresh coriander (*dhaniya*)

4-5 almonds, chopped

4-5 raisins

4-5 pistachios, chopped

4 Tbsp gram flour (*besan*)

Salt, to taste

5-6 Tbsp refined oil

FOR THE GRAVY:

100 g cashews, ground into a paste

2 Tbsp refined oil

2 Tbsp butter

1 Tbsp ginger-garlic paste (p. 21)

½ kg medium-sized onions, boiled and cooled

½ kg tomatoes, made to a paste (p. 21)

1 tsp turmeric (*haldi*) powder

1 tsp garam masala (p. 16)

1 tsp red chilli (*lal mirch*) powder

1 Tbsp Shahi Paneer masala (store bought)

1 Tbsp milk

METHOD

TO MAKE THE STUFFED PANEER:

1. Slit each piece of paneer down the middle but not all the way through, keeping one side intact. Set aside on a flat plate.
2. In a blender jar, add the cashews and fresh coriander, and blend at medium setting to make a thick paste. Transfer into a bowl.
3. Add the almonds, raisins, and pistachios to the cashew paste and combine well.
4. Take a portion of this mixture and stuff the paneer, ensuring the paneer pieces do not break.
5. In a separate bowl, combine the gram flour with 2 Tbsp water and ½ tsp salt to make a thick batter.
6. Heat the oil in a frying pan over high heat. Once hot, reduce the heat to medium.
7. Dip each piece of stuffed paneer in the batter and fry in small batches until golden brown on both sides. Use a slotted spoon and transfer to a serving bowl. Set aside.

TO MAKE THE GRAVY:

8. Add the cashews and 2 tsp water to a blender jar to make a thick paste.
9. In a wok over medium heat, add the oil and butter. Once hot, add the ginger-garlic paste and sauté for 2-3 minutes.
10. Add the cashew paste, boiled onions, tomato paste and sauté for 2 to 3 minutes, until the oil separates and rises to the surface.
11. Reduce the heat and add turmeric, garam masala, red chilli powder, shahi paneer masala, and season to taste with salt. Simmer for 15 to 20 minutes.
12. Increase the heat to medium-high. Add the milk and bring to a boil.
13. Now reduce the heat and cover the wok with a lid. Cook for about 2 to 3 minutes. Remove from heat but keep covered until before serving.
14. Pour the gravy over the prepared stuffed paneer to submerge it completely and serve hot with roomali rotis (p. 157).

COOKING TIME: **60 MINUTES**

SERVES: **4-5**

PALAK AUR METHI ALOO

Dry dish of potatoes and spinach cooked to perfection

INGREDIENTS

30 ml mustard oil

1 tsp cumin seeds (*jeera sabut*)

1 onion, chopped

500 g fenugreek leaves (*methi*), washed and chopped

1 potato (*aloo*), chopped

500 g spinach (*palak*), washed and chopped

1 dry red chilli (*sookhi lal mirch*)

8-10 garlic cloves

1 tsp coriander (*dhaniya*) powder

1 tsp turmeric (*haldi*) powder

1 tsp garam masala (p. 16)

½ tsp salt, or to taste

1 tsp red chilli (*lal mirch*) powder

METHOD

1. Heat the oil in a wok over high heat for 2-3 minutes. Once the oil turns smoky, reduce the heat to medium. Add the cumin seeds and roast for 2 minutes.
2. Add the onions and sauté until pink.
3. Add the fenugreek leaves, potatoes, spinach, dry red chilli, garlic, coriander powder, turmeric powder, garam masala, salt, and red chilli powder. Cover the wok with a lid and cook over low heat, stirring frequently.
4. Cook for 15-20 minutes until the preparation dries out. Serve hot with roomali rotis (p. 157).

COOKING TIME: **40-45 MINUTES**

SERVES: **3-4**

PYAAJ KARELA

Bitter gourd with onions

INGREDIENTS

1 kg bitter gourd (*karela*)

Salt, to taste

90 ml mustard oil

3 medium-sized onions, sliced

1 tsp cumin seeds (*jeera sabut*)

2-4 green chillies (*hari mirch*), chopped

½ Tbsp chaat masala (p. 17)

METHOD

1. Peel and deseed the bitter gourd. Chop into small pieces and rub all over with salt. Set aside for 10-15 minutes.
2. In a cooking pot over medium heat, boil the salted bitter gourd in 1½ litres water for 15-20 minutes. Remove from heat and drain the water.
3. Now add fresh water (1½ litres) to the pot and boil the bitter gourd again for 15-20 minutes. Let the water cool and squeeze out of the bitter gourd by hand. Spread over a muslin cloth to dry.
4. In a wok over high heat, add 2 Tbsp oil and heat for 2 to 3 minutes. Once the oil turns smoky, reduce the heat to medium and add the bitter gourds. Sauté for 5 to 10 minutes, or until it turns pale. Use a slotted spoon and drain out on kitchen towels. Set aside.
5. In the same wok, add the remaining oil. Once hot, add the onions and cumin seeds; sauté until the onions turn light pink.
6. Add the sautéd bitter gourd and cook over medium heat until tender by covering it when done.
7. Add the green chillies and chaat masala. Stir well and remove from heat.
8. Serve hot with chappatis (p. 168).

COOKING TIME: **40-45 MINUTES**

SERVES: **6-8**

BAINGAN BHARTA

Smoky roasted eggplant

INGREDIENTS

1 kg round eggplants

8 Tbsp refined oil

1 Tbsp cumin seeds (*jeera sabut*)

2 green chillies (*hari mirch*), slit

4 large onions, chopped

4-5 medium-sized tomatoes, chopped

1 tsp red chilli pepper (*degi mirch)* powder

Salt, to taste

Fresh coriander (*dhaniya*), to garnish

METHOD

1. Roast the eggplants on a grill or over an open flame until they are completely cooked and the peel turns charred and crunchy. Once cool, peel and mash it on a flat plate with a fork.
2. Heat the oil in a wok over high heat. Add the cumin seeds and green chillies and roast for 1 to 2 minutes.
3. Add the chopped onions and sauté until brown.
4. Add the tomatoes and cook for 5 minutes whilst stirring continously.
5. Add the red chilli pepper powder and season to taste with salt. Cook until the tomatoes are soft and oil oozes out from the preparation.
6. Now add the mashed eggplant and mix well. Cook over medium heat for 5 to 8 minutes.
7. Remove from heat and garnish with fresh coriander leaves. Serve with chappatis (p. 154).

COOKING TIME: **40-45 MINUTES**

SERVES: **4-5**

TOOTMAAR ALOO

Crumbled potatoes in a flavourful curry

INGREDIENTS

30 ml refined oil

½ tsp cumin seeds (*jeera sabut*)

2 medium-sized onions, chopped

3 medium-sized tomatoes, chopped

1 Tbsp ginger-garlic paste (p. 21)

1 tsp turmeric (*haldi*) powder

1 tsp red chilli (*lal mirch*) powder

1 tsp coriander (*dhaniya*) powder

1 tsp garam masala (p. 16)

4 green chillies (*hari mirch*), lengthwise

Salt, to taste

½ kg medium-sized potatoes, boiled and crumbled

1 Tbsp dried fenugreek leaves (*kasoori methi*)

1 tsp chaat masala (p. 17)

METHOD

1. Heat the oil in a wok over high heat. Add the cumin seeds and cook for 1 minute until it starts to splutter.
2. Reduce the heat to medium-low and add the chopped onions. Sauté until they are light pink.
3. Add the tomatoes, ginger-garlic paste, turmeric, red chilli powder, coriander powder, garam masala, and green chillies. Season to taste with salt.
4. Add the potatoes and 1½ cups of water and simmer over high heat for 8 to 10 minutes. The water should reduce to half its quantity.
5. Sprinkle the dried fenugreek leaves and chaat masala and remove the wok from heat.
6. Cover the wok with a lid and remove it just before serving with tandoori rotis (p. 156).

COOKING TIME: **30-35 MINUTES**

SERVES: **5-6**

KADDU SABZI AUR PYAAZ CHUTNEY

Pumpkin curry paired with onion chutney

INGREDIENTS

1 kg pumpkin (*kaddu*)

1 ltr water

60 ml mustard oil

1 tsp cumin seeds (*jeera sabut*)

2 medium-sized onions, chopped

3 medium-sized tomatoes, roasted and mashed

1 Tbsp ginger-garlic paste (p. 31)

1 tsp turmeric (*haldi*) powder

1 tsp coriander (*dhaniya*) powder

1 tsp red chilli pepper (*degi mirch*) powder

1 tsp garam masala (p. 16)

Salt, to taste

1 Tbsp tamarind paste (p. 23)

½ tsp roasted cumin (*jeera*) powder

4-6 green chillies (*hari mirch*), chopped

100 g fresh coriander (*dhaniya*)

FOR THE ONION CHUTNEY:

2 Tbsp mustard oil

6 medium-sized onions, sliced

4 green chillies (*hari mirch*), slit

½ tsp turmeric (*haldi*) powder

Salt, to taste

½ Tbsp lemon juice

COOKING TIME: **60 MINUTES**

METHOD

1. Peel the pumpkin and chop into small cubes. Add it to a pressure cooker with 1 litre water and lock the lid in place. Pressure cook over medium heat for 2-3 whistles. Open the lid once the pressure releases on its own. Use a slotted spoon and transfer the pumpkin to a bowl. Mash it roughly with a ladle.
2. Heat the oil in a wok over high heat for 2-3 minutes, or until it is smoky. Reduce the heat to medium and add the cumin seeds. Cook until the seeds splutter.
3. Reduce the heat to medium-low and add the onions. Sauté until they are light pink.
4. Stir in the tomatoes, ginger-garlic paste, turmeric, coriander powder, red chilli pepper powder, garam masala, and season to taste with salt. Sauté over high heat for 5 minutes or until the oil separates.
5. Now add the mashed pumpkin and cover the wok with a lid. Cook over medium heat for 10 minutes. If the pumpkin dries out, add a dash of water and cover again.
6. Add the tamarind paste and cumin powder.
7. Remove from heat once the pumpkin is dry and the water has evaporated. Garnish with green chilli and fresh coriander.

TO MAKE THE ONION CHUTNEY:

8. In a pan over high heat, add the oil. Once it turns smoky, reduce the heat to medium-low.
9. Add the onions and sauté until they are soft.
10. Add the green chillies, turmeric, and season to taste with salt. Cook for another 5 minutes. Remove from heat, and add the lime juice. Cover the pan.
11. Remove the cover and reheat it before serving it with the kaddu sabzi and besan rotis (p. 159).

SERVES: **6-8**

ALOO KATLI

Crispy spiced dry potatoes

INGREDIENTS

1 kg medium-sized potatoes

6 Tbsp mustard oil

1 tsp cumin seeds (*jeera sabut*)

6-7 dry red chillies (*sookhi lal mirch*), chopped

1 large onion, sliced

½ tsp red chilli pepper (*degi mirch*) powder

Salt, to taste

2 green chillies (*hari mirch*), chopped

50 g fresh coriander (*dhaniya*), chopped

METHOD

1. Rinse, peel, and slice the potatoes into round quarter-inch thick slices to ensure the potatoes are thick enough to cook.
2. Heat the oil in a wok over high heat until smoky. Reduce the heat to medium and add the cumin seeds; roast until they splutter.
3. Reduce the heat to medium-low. Add the dry red chillies and onions and sauté until soft.
4. Add the potatoes, red chilli pepper powder, green chillies, and season to taste with salt. Cover the wok with a lid and cook over low heat for 5 minutes.
5. Remove the lid and flip the potatoes to allow them to cook on the other side. The potato slices should be soft, tender, and golden brown on both the sides.
6. Remove from heat, and garnish with fresh coriander. This dish is best enjoyed with sheermal (p. 161).

COOKING TIME: **30-35 MINUTES**

SERVES: **4-6**

MATAR KALA TIL

Stir-fry of vibrant green peas and black sesame seeds

INGREDIENTS

500 g fresh or frozen peas

½ ltr water

30 ml sesame oil

2 tsp black sesame seeds (*kala til*)

Salt, to taste

METHOD

1. In a pan over medium heat, boil the peas in ½ litre water for 25-30 minutes or until they're soft. Strain and set aside.
2. Heat the oil in a sauté pan over medium heat for 2-3 minutes. Add the boiled peas, black sesame seeds and sauté for 7-8 minutes, stirring occassionally.
3. Season to taste with salt. Remove the pan from heat and keep covered until served hot.

COOKING TIME: **30 MINUTES**

SERVES: **3-4**

BINA HAPPA

The ultimate comfort food – urad dal khichdi

INGREDIENTS

350 g basmati rice

150 g black lentils (*sabut urad dal*)

50 ml refined oil

1 tsp cumin seeds (*jeera sabut*)

1 medium-sized onion, sliced

1 tsp ginger-garlic paste (p. 21)

3-4 green chillies (*hari mirch*), chopped

Salt, to taste

METHOD

1. Wash the rice and lentils thoroughly in running water.
2. In a large bowl, soak the rice and lentils together in enough water to submerge them completely for 90 minutes.
3. Heat the oil in a pressure cooker over medium heat for 2-3 minutes. Add the cumin seeds and roast until they splutter.
4. Add the onions and sauté until brown.
5. Now add the ginger-garlic paste and green chillies, and sauté for 2-3 minutes.
6. Add 5 cups of water and bring to a boil.
7. Drain the rice and lentils add to the cooker. Season to taste with salt and close the lid. Pressure cook over high heat for 2-3 whistles.
8. Reduce the heat to low and cook for another 10 minutes. Remove from heat and let the pressure release. Open the lid and make sure the water has dried and the khichdi is of thick consistency.
9. Serve with yoghurt/butter/ghee.

COOKING TIME: **30 MINUTES**

SERVES: **4-5**

RAMPURI DAL

A traditional black gram preparation from Rampur

INGREDIENTS

½ kg whole washed black gram (*urad dal* without husk)

1 ltr water

30 ml refined oil

1 Tbsp yellow butter

Pinch of asafoetida (*hing*)

1 tsp cumin seeds (*jeera sabut*)

1 medium-sized onion, chopped

4 dry whole red chillies (*sookhi lal mirch*), halved

4-6 (1") pieces ginger, chopped

6-8 green chillies (*hari mirch*), chopped

Salt, to taste

1 tsp chaat masala (p. 17)

1 lemon, juiced

50 g fresh coriander (*dhaniya*), chopped

METHOD

1. Wash the dal thoroughly in running water.
2. In a medium-size bowl, soak the dal in cold water until it is completely submerged for 10-15 minutes. Drain excess water and transfer it to a cooking pot over high heat. Add 1 litre water and bring to a boil. Simmer for 30 minutes until the dal softens.
3. Heat the oil and butter in a wok over medium heat. Add the asafoetida, cumin seeds and onion, and sauté until the onions turn light pink.
4. Add the dry red chillies and ginger. Stir well and cook for another 2-3 minutes.
5. Now add the boiled dal, green chillies, and season to taste with salt. Sprinkle the chaat masala, and add lemon juice, and fresh coriander. Simmer over low heat for 5 minutes. Serve hot with roomali rotis (p. 157).

COOKING TIME: **60 MINUTES**

SERVES: **6-8**

KARELA WITH CHANA DAL

Bitter gourd with Bengal gram

INGREDIENTS

150 g Bengal gram (*chana dal*)

1 kg bitter gourd (*karela*)

4 Tbsp + 4 Tbsp refined oil

1 tsp black mustard seeds

2 medium-sized onions, chopped

2 medium-sized tomatoes, chopped

1 tsp turmeric powder (*haldi*)

Salt, to taste

10-12 curry patta leaves

1 lemon, juiced

2-3 green chillies, chopped

1 Tbsp fresh coriander leaves

METHOD

1. Wash the chana dal thoroughly and soak in 2 cups of water for an hour.
2. In a pressure cooker over medium heat, add the soaked dal with water and cook for 2 to 3 whistles. Remove from heat and let the pressure release.
3. Open the lid and check the dal for doneness. Drain the dal and keep aside.
4. Peel the bitter gourd and remove the seeds. Chop it into fine pieces like kuchumber. Transfer them to a large bowl and soak in cold water for 30 minutes.
5. Heat 4 Tbsp oil in a wok over medium heat.
6. Add the mustard seeds and let them crackle for 1-2 minutes. Add the onion and sauté to light brown.
7. Add the tomatoes and curry leaves. Saute until the tomatoes are tender. Now sprinkle turmeric and season to taste with salt. Stir well to combine.
8. As the masala cooks and the oil separates, add the boiled dal and cook for 15-20 minutes. Remove from heat and cover the wok with a lid.
9. Squeeze the bitter gourd to remove any excess water. Now, in a pot over medium heat, add fresh water and bitter gourd. Boil for 5-10 minutes.
10. Drain the bitter gourd in a colander. Add fresh water to the pot and boil again over medium heat. This is important to remove the bitterness of the vegetable.
11. Squeeze the bitter gourd and leave to dry on a muslin cloth.
12. In a large pan over medium heat, add 3/4 Tbsp oil. Add the bitter gourd and sauté for 10 minutes until light brown on the edges. Remove from heat.
13. Now, return the wok with the dal over medium heat and transfer the bitter gourd to combine with it. Cook over medium heat for 5-6 minutes. Add the lemon juice and stir well to combine.
14. Garnish with fresh coriander and green chillies. Serve with hot chappati (p. 154).

COOKING TIME: **60 MINUTES**

SERVES: **5-6**

KADHAI DAL

Spicy and flavourful lentil stew

INGREDIENTS

500 g split black gram (*urad chilka dal*)

1 ltr water

Salt, to taste

½ cup refined oil

4 medium-sized onions, chopped

4 medium-sized tomatoes, chopped

1 tsp black pepper (*kali mirch*) powder

1 tsp red chilli pepper (*degi mirch*) powder

1 tsp dried fenugreek leaves (*kasoori methi*)

1 tsp MDH Kitchen King masala (mixed spice blend)

Salt, to taste

1 (1") piece ginger, julienned

2-3 green chillies (*hari mirch*), for garnish

METHOD

1. Wash the dal thoroughly in running water.
2. In a cooking pot over high heat, add the dal and 1 litre water. Season to taste with salt and bring to a boil. Simmer for about 15-20 minutes. Drain the excess water using a sieve and set the dal aside.
3. Heat the oil in a wok over high heat. Once the oil turns smoky, reduce the heat to medium and add onions. Sauté until they turn translucent.
4. Add the tomatoes and cook until they soften and the oil separates.
5. Now add the boiled dal and stir gently, ensuring it does not become mushy.
6. Add the black pepper powder, red chilli pepper powder, dried fenugreek leaves. Add the Kitchen King masala. Season to taste with salt and let the dal simmer for about 5-10 minutes. Remove from heat.
7. Garnish with ginger and green chillies, and serve hot with tandoori rotis (p. 156).

COOKING TIME: **45 MINUTES**

SERVES: **4-5**

MAINS
POULTRY, MUTTON & FISH

EGG CURRY

Spicy and aromatic egg curry

INGREDIENTS

2 Tbsp refined oil

2 medium-sized onions, made to a paste (p. 22)

2 green chillies (*hari mirch*), chopped

1 Tbsp ginger-garlic paste (p. 21)

2 medium-sized tomatoes, made to a paste (p. 21)

1 tsp turmeric (*haldi*) powder

1 tsp red chilli pepper (*degi mirch*) powder

1 tsp coriander (*dhaniya*) powder

½ tsp red chilli (*lal mirch*) powder

½ tsp garam masala (p. 16)

Salt, to taste

6 eggs, hard boiled, peeled

1 tsp dried fenugreek leaves (*kasoori methi*)

50 g fresh coriander (*dhaniya*), chopped

METHOD

1. Heat 1 Tbsp oil in a wok over medium heat for 2-3 minutes.
2. Add the onion paste and green chillies, and fry until the onion paste turns golden brown.
3. Add the ginger-garlic paste and sauté for 2-3 minutes.
4. Add the tomato paste, turmeric, red chilli pepper powder, coriander powder, red chilli powder, garam masala, and season to taste with salt. Cook until the oil separates on the side of the pan.
5. Depending on the required consistency, pour enough water into the wok and cook over high heat. Stir until the curry thickens to your desired consistency.
6. Heat the remaining oil in a broad pan over medium heat. Make sure the boiled eggs are dry and prink them with fork 2/3 times. Now add the eggs and gently fry until golden and blistered.
7. Add the fried eggs and dried fenugreek leaves to the wok with the curry and simmer for 2-4 minutes.
8. Remove from heat and garnish with fresh coriander at the time of serving. Serve hot with roomali rotis (p. 157).

COOKING TIME: **35-40 MINUTES**

SERVES: **4-5**

KHOGINA

Indian-style scrambled eggs

INGREDIENTS

45 ml butter/olive oil

2 onions, chopped

1 tomato, chopped

1 tsp turmeric (*haldi*) powder

1 tsp red chilli pepper (*degi mirch*) powder

1 tsp coriander (*dhaniya*) powder

1 tsp red chilli (*lal mirch*) powder

6 eggs

Salt, to taste

Fresh coriander (*dhaniya*), chopped

1 green chilli (*hari mirch*), chopped

METHOD

1. In a fry pan over medium heat, add the butter and tilt the pan from side to side so that the pan is coated evenly.
2. Add the onions and fry until they soften and turn golden brown.
3. Add the tomato, turmeric, chilli pepper powder, coriander powder, and red chilli powder. Reduce the heat and stir well. Cook until the tomatoes are soft. Remove the pan from heat.
4. In a medium-size bowl, crack the eggs, add salt and whisk lightly.
5. Add the fresh coriander and green chilli, and continue to whisk.
6. Now return the pan with fried onion and tomatoes to medium heat and add the whisked eggs.
7. Stir for 5-7 minutes to achieve a soft custard-like consistency. Keep scraping the bottom and sides of the pan.
8. Remove from heat and serve hot with chappatis (p. 154).

COOKING TIME: **20-25 MINUTES**

SERVES: **4-5**

OMELETTE CURRY

Omelette in a velvety curry

INGREDIENTS

FOR THE OMELETTE:

6 eggs

5 g fresh coriander (*dhaniya*), chopped

1 large onion, chopped

1 medium-sized tomato, chopped

2 green chillies (*hari mirch*), chopped

Salt, to taste

4 Tbsp refined oil

FOR THE GRAVY:

½ tsp cumin (*jeera*) powder

1 medium-sized tomato, chopped

5-6 garlic cloves, chopped

10 g ginger

4 green chillies (*hari mirch*), chopped

1 dry red chilli (*sookhi lal mirch*)

1 cinnamon (*dal chini*) stick

7-8 peppercorns (*kali mirch*)

1 tsp coriander seeds (*dhaniya sabut*)

5 Tbsp refined oil

1 tsp cumin seeds (*jeera sabut*)

2-3 bay leaves (*tej patta*)

1 large onion, finely chopped

1 tsp turmeric (*haldi*) powder

Salt, to taste

COOKING TIME: **40 MINUTES**

METHOD

1. In a large bowl, crack the eggs. Add the fresh coriander, onion, tomato, green chillies, and season to taste with salt. Whisk them well to ensure they remain fluffy.
2. In a broad pan over medium heat, add 4 tablespoons of oil and heat for 2 minutes. Add the whisked egg mixture and let it cook evenly for 2-3 minutes until one side is fully done. Flip the omelette and cook the other side.
3. Remove from heat, and cut the omelette into cubes. Set aside.
4. In a grinder jar, add the cumin powder, tomato, garlic, ginger, green chillies, red chilli, cinnamon, peppercorns, and coriander seeds. Grind at a medium setting for 2-3 minutes to make a paste, adding water if required.
5. Heat the oil in a wok over medium heat for 2-3 minutes. Add the cumin seeds and bay leaves and wait until they splutter.
6. Add the chopped onions and sauté until lightly browned.
7. Now add the prepared spice paste, turmeric, and season to taste with salt. For the curry, add 2 cups of water and bring to a boil. Cover the wok with a lid and simmer for 10 minutes.
8. Remove the lid and add the cubed omelette pieces. Cover the wok again and simmer for another 2 minutes.
9. Remove from heat and set aside to allow the flavours to meld. Serve hot.

SERVES: **5-6**

CHICKEN ISHTEW

Hearty chicken dish with aromatic spices

INGREDIENTS

150 g ghee

8 medium-sized onions, sliced

1 tsp cumin seeds (*jeera sabut*)

1 kg bone-in chicken, cut into 12-14 pieces

1 Tbsp chopped ginger

1 Tbsp chopped garlic

2 (1-inch) cinnamon (*dal chini*) sticks

6 green cardamom (*hari elaichi*) pods

4 black cardamom (*moti elaichi*) pods

2 star anise (*chakri ke phool*)

6 cloves (*laung*)

4 bay leaves (*tej patta*)

Salt, to taste

6 whole dry red chillies (*sookhi sabut lal mirch*)

½ cup refined oil

150 g yoghurt (*dahi*)

1 tsp chaat masala (p. 17)

1 lemon, quartered

6-8 green chillies (*hari mirch*), chopped

COOKING TIME: **60 MINUTES**

METHOD

1. Heat the ghee in a wok over high heat for 2-3 minutes. Reduce the heat to medium. Add 2 sliced onions and sauté until they soften. Add the cumin seeds and roast until they splutter.
2. Now add the chicken pieces, ginger, garlic, cinnamon sticks, green cardamom, black cardamom, star anise, cloves, and bay leaves. Stir well to combine.
3. Season to taste with salt and add the whole dry red chillies. Cook for 8-10 minutes over high heat, stirring continuously.
4. In a separate wok, heat the oil over medium heat. Add the remaining onions and sauté until light pink. Add the chicken mix and yoghurt. Roast over medium heat until the chicken is tender.
5. Garnish with chaat masala, lemon, and green chillies. Remove from heat and serve hot with roomali rotis (p. 157).

SERVES: **4-6**

CHICKEN BURRAH

Slow-cooked marinated chicken

INGREDIENTS

500-700 g bone-in chicken

FOR THE MARINADE:

2 Tbsp ginger-garlic paste (p. 21)

2 tsp brown onion paste

1 tsp red chilli (*lal mirch*) powder

1 tsp cumin (*jeera*) powder

1 tsp garam masala (p. 16)

½ tsp cinnamon (*dal chini*) powder

1 tsp black pepper (*kali mirch*) powder

2 Tbsp butter

400 g yoghurt (*dahi*)

2 lemons, juiced

1 Tbsp oil

½ tsp food colour (optional)

3-4 Tbsp oil, to grill

FOR THE GRAVY:

4 Tbsp refined oil

3 tsp ginger-garlic paste

2 large onions, paste, fried

2 green chillies, chopped

5-6 tomatoes, pureed (p. 22)

1 tsp red chilli powder

1 tsp cumin (*jeera*) powder

1 tsp garam masala

1 tsp cinnamon (*dal chini*) powder

2 tsp dried fenugreek leaves (*kasoori methi*)

Salt, to taste

200 g cashew paste

100 g yoghurt (*dahi*)

150 g fresh cream

2 Tbsp milk

COOKING TIME: **60 MINUTES**

METHOD

1. In a large bowl, combine the ingredients for the marinade; rub the mixture all over the chicken and marinate in the refigerator for an hour.
2. In a grilling pan over medium heat, heat 3-4 Tbsp oil. Add the marinated chicken, ensuring that you save any marinade left in the bowl. Grill all sides of the chicken until golden brown. Set aside.

TO MAKE THE GRAVY:

3. Heat the oil in a wok over medium heat. Add the ginger-garlic paste and cook for 2 minutes.
4. Add the fried onion paste and green chillies, and cook for 3-4 minutes.
5. Add the tomato puree and stir well.
6. Add the red chilli powder, cumin powder, garam masala, cinnamon powder, dried fenugreek leaves, and season to taste with salt. Simmer for 10 minutes, stirring frequently.
7. Stir in the cashew paste and cook until the oil separates and rises to the surface.
8. Add the yoghurt and stir well. Simmer for 5-10 minutes.
9. Now add the cream and bring to a boil. Add the milk and any remaining marinade.
10. Add the grilled chicken to the gravy and simmer for 10 minutes.
11. In a small bowl, burn a small piece of charcoal. Create a well in the centre of the wok and place the bowl of burning charcoal in it. Cover the wok with a lid and cook for 3 minutes to smoke the dish.
12. Remove from heat and serve hot with roomali rotis (p. 157).

SERVES: **4-5**

CHICKEN NIHARI

Slow-cooked chicken curry tempered with ghee and spices

INGREDIENTS

300 ml refined oil

1 kg bone-in chicken, cut into 12-14 pieces

60 g Nihari masala (p. 19) or store bought masala

2 Tbsp ginger-garlic paste (p. 21)

2 Tbsp chilli pepper (*degi mirch*) powder

4 medium-sized onions, sliced, fried, cooled and ground

Salt, to taste

100 g wheat flour (*atta*), roasted

FOR TEMPERING:

300 g ghee

1 (1") piece ginger, julienned

½ tsp red chilli pepper (*degi mirch*) powder

FOR THE GARNISH:

1 lemon, sliced or cut into wedges

2 green chillies, chopped

1 (1") ginger, julienned

25 g gresh coriander

2 Tbsp fried onions

METHOD

1. Heat the oil in a cooking pot over high heat. Add the chicken pieces.
2. Add the Nihari masala, ginger-garlic paste, chilli pepper powder, and cook for 30 minutes over high heat. Stir occasionally.
3. Add the fried onions and season to taste with salt. Stir frequently and cook for 2-3 minutes.
4. Add 4-5 cups of water and bring to a boil.
5. Reduce the heat to low and add the roasted wheat flour. Let simmer for 30 minutes, whilst stirring occasionally.
6. Cook until the chicken is tender and the oil separates.
7. For tempering, heat the ghee in a tadka pan over high heat. Add the ginger and red chilli pepper powder, sauté for 2-3 minutes and pour over the nihari.
8. Garnish with lemon wedges, green chillies, ginger strips, coriander, and fried onions. Serve hot with tandoori rotis (p. 156).

COOKING TIME: **90 MINUTES**

SERVES: **6-8**

CHICKEN KORMA

Aromatic and spicy chicken curry

INGREDIENTS

200 g ghee

3 medium-sized onions, sliced

150 g korma masala (store bought)

1 kg bone-in chicken, cut into 12-14 pieces

1 Tbsp ginger-garlic paste (p. 21)

Salt, to taste

1 tsp Kashmiri chilli (*Kashmiri mirch*) powder

1 tsp red chilli pepper (*degi mirch*) powder

1 tsp turmeric (*haldi*) powder

1 tsp coriander (*dhaniya*) powder

2 onions, sliced, fried, cooled and ground

1 tsp chaat masala (p. 17)

1 tsp garam masala (p. 16)

METHOD

1. In a wok over medium heat, add the ghee and sliced onions, and sauté until they turn pink.
2. Add the korma masala, chicken, ginger-garlic paste, and season with salt. Stir well.
3. Add the Kashmiri chilli powder, red chilli pepper powder, turmeric, and coriander powder. Stir well and cook for 8-10 minutes over high heat.
4. Reduce the heat to medium and add fried onions. Cook for another 10 minutes, stirring frequently.
5. Now add 3-4 cups of water and simmer for 15-20 minutes until the chicken is tender and the gravy thickens.
6. Sprinkle the chaat masala and garam masala. Mix well.
7. Remove from heat and cover it until before serving. Serve hot with roomali rotis (p. 157).

COOKING TIME: **60 MINUTES**

SERVES: **6-8**

CHICKEN KADHAI

Semi-dry chicken dish

INGREDIENTS

200 ml refined oil

1 kg bone-in chicken, cut into 12-14 pieces

1 tsp white pepper (*safed mirch*) powder

Salt, to taste

1 large tomato, chopped

1 tsp red chilli pepper (*degi mirch*) powder

3 tsp yoghurt

2 Tbsp sliced garlic

2 Tbsp julienned ginger

6-8 large green chillies (*hari mirch*), chopped into 3-4 pieces each

50 g fresh coriander (*dhaniya*), chopped

METHOD

1. Heat the oil in a wok over high heat for 2 minutes. Add the chicken, white pepper, and season to taste with salt. Cook for 5 minutes.
2. Add the tomato and chilli pepper powder, and stir well. Now cover the wok with a lid and cook for 10-12 minutes, stirring occasionally.
3. Remove the lid and when the tomatoes dry up, add the yoghurt, garlic, ginger, green chillies, and coriander.
4. Cover the wok again and cook for 2-3 minutes. Remove from heat and serve hot with tandoori rotis (p. 156).

COOKING TIME: **60 MINUTES**

SERVES: **4-5**

BUTTER CHICKEN

Creamy, tomato-based chicken curry – a classic Indian comfort dish

INGREDIENTS

FOR BONELESS BUTTER CHICKEN:

2 kg boneless chicken, cut into 24-28 pieces

FOR BONE-IN BUTTER CHICKEN:

2 thigh pieces of chicken, 500-700 g each

250 g yoghurt (*dahi*)

2 Tbsp ginger-garlic paste (p. 21)

2 Tbsp refined oil

1 tsp red chilli pepper (*degi mirch*) powder

½ tsp red chilli (*lal mirch*) powder

Pinch of edible red colour

4 tsp garam masala (p. 16)

Salt, to taste

3 Tbsp ghee

200 g unsalted cashew nuts (*kaju*)

300 g yellow butter

400 g tomato puree (p. 22)

400 g cream

5 large green chillies (*hari mirch*), slit and deseeded

1 ltr milk

1½ tsp sugar

2 Tbsp dried fenugreek leaves (*kasoori methi*)

METHOD

1. Marinate the chicken in a marinade of yoghurt, ginger-garlic paste, refined oil, chilli pepper powder, red chilli powder, red colour, 2 tsp garam masala, and some salt. Set aside for 1 hour.
2. In a large bowl, add the marinated chicken and create a gap in the centre.
3. In a small bowl, add ½ Tbsp ghee or butter. Burn a small piece of charcoal and place it in the bowl with the butter. Place this bowl in the centre of the large bowl with the marinated chicken and cover for 3 minutes to smoke the meat.
4. Thread the smoked chicken pieces onto skewers.
5. Heat ½ tsp ghee (for 4 pieces) in a grilling pan over high heat for 2-3 minutes. Remove the skewered chunks and transfer onto the grilling pan. Cook for 8-10 minutes until the meat turns golden brown and then flip the meat and cook the other side. Repeat the process for the remaining pieces.

FOR THE CASHEW PASTE:

6. Soak the cashew nuts in a bowl of water for 30 minutes. They should be completely submerged in water. Drain and transfer them to a blender jar.
7. Blend at medium setting for 2-3 minutes until the cashews turn into a smooth paste.

FOR THE GRAVY:

8. In a wok over high heat, add the butter and cashew paste. Cook for 5-10 minutes until the paste turns golden brown.
9. Add the tomato puree and sauté for 10 minutes.
10. Add the cream and green chillies and cook for 10 minutes over high heat. Add the milk, sugar, 2 tsp garam masala, and season to taste with salt.
11. Rub the dried fenugreek leaves between your palms until they turn flaky and powdery and add to the wok.
12. Reduce the heat to low and add the roasted chicken. Let simmer for another 10 minutes.
13. Remove from heat, and cover until serving to allow the flavours to meld together. Serve with hot sesame naan (p. 155).

COOKING TIME: **60 MINUTES**

SERVES: **4-6**

CHICKEN KEEMA

Flavourful minced chicken

INGREDIENTS

1 kg minced chicken (*keema*)

100 ml refined oil

3 medium-sized onions, thinly sliced

4 cloves (*laung*)

4 green cardamom (*hari elaichi*) pods

5 peppercorns (*kali mirch*)

2 bay leaves (*tej patta*)

2 tsp garlic paste

2 tsp ginger paste

Salt, to taste

2 Tbsp yoghurt (*dahi*)

2-3 green chillies (*hari mirch*), julienned

METHOD

1. Wash the keema in a fine-mesh strainer and keep aside to drain.
2. Heat the oil in a pressure cooker over medium heat. Once it begins to simmer, add the sliced onions and cook until they turn light brown.
3. Add the cloves, cardamom pods, peppercorns, and bay leaves. Reduce the heat to low and stir for 2-3 minutes.
4. Add the chicken keema, garlic and ginger paste. Stir well.
5. Season to taste with salt and add the yoghurt. Stir well for 3 minutes.
6. Close the lid of the pressure cooker and increase the heat to high. Pressure-cook for one whistle.
7. Now reduce the heat to low and cook for 8-10 minutes for 2 more whistles. Remove the cooker from heat.
8. Let the pressure release and open the lid. Garnish with green chillies at the time of serving with hot chappatis (p. 154).

COOKING TIME: **45 MINUTES**

SERVES: **6**

CHICKEN KAALI MIRCH

Chicken curry with black pepper

INGREDIENTS

250 ml yoghurt (*dahi*)

500-600 g bone-in chicken

250 ml milk

500 g dairy fresh cream (not packet cream)

1 Tbsp coconut powder

1 Tbsp dried fenugreek leaves (*kasoori methi*)

1 tsp salt, or to taste

2 medium-sized onions, sliced, fried, cooled and ground with a splash of water

1 Tbsp black pepper, crushed

1 tsp chaat masala (p. 17)

1 tsp dried mango powder (*amchur*)

½ tsp coriander powder (*dhaniya* powder)

½ tsp cumin powder (*jeera*)

6 green chillies (*hari mirch*), slit

1 (2") piece ginger, julienned

WHOLE SPICES:

2 black cardamom (*moti elaichi*) pods

4-5 cloves (*laung*)

METHOD

1. In a cooking pot over medium heat, add the yoghurt, chicken, milk, cream, coconut powder, dried fenugreek leaves, salt, 1 tsp browned onions, black pepper, chaat masala, mango powder, coriander powder, and cumin powder. Stir well to combine.
2. Cook for 1 hour, stirring occasionally.
3. When it begins to dry, add the slit green chillies and ginger.
4. Using a mortar and pestle, finely crush the black cardamoms and cloves. Add them into the pot.
5. Remove from heat and cover until ready to serve. Serve hot with roomali rotis (p. 157).

COOKING TIME: **80 MINUTES**

SERVES: **4-6**

MURGH MUSSALAM WITH GRAVY

Slow-cooked stuffed chicken with gravy

INGREDIENTS

FOR THE BRINE:

900 g whole chicken

½ cup vinegar

1 Tbsp salt

FOR THE MARINADE:

1 Tbsp ginger-garlic paste (p. 21)

1 tsp red chilli (*lal mirch*) powder

2-3 Tbsp yoghurt (*dahi*)

2 tsp Kashmiri red chilli (*Kashmiri lal mirch*) powder

Salt, to taste

1 tsp chaat masala (p. 17)

1 tsp cumin (*jeera*) powder

2-3 tsp lemon juice

1 tsp garam masala (p. 16)

FOR THE DRIED FRUIT PASTE:

10-12 cashew nuts

10-12 almonds

1 mace (*javitri*)

4-5 green cardamom (*hari elaichi*) pods

1 Tbsp Cuddapah almond (*chironji*)

1 tsp poppy seeds (*khus khus*), optional

4-5 cloves (*laung*)

FOR THE GRAVY:

3-4 Tbsp refined oil

1" cinnamon stick (*dal chini*)

2 medium-sized onions, finely chopped

1 Tbsp ginger-garlic paste

1 tsp red chilli pepper (*degi mirch*) powder

1 tsp salt

½ tsp garam masala

1 tsp coriander (*dhaniya*) powder

1 Tbsp cumin seeds (*jeera sabut*), roasted

2 tomatoes, made to a paste (p. 21)

½ cup yoghurt (*dahi*)

10-12 strands of saffron, soaked in water for 5-10 minutes prior to use

½ cup chopped fresh coriander (*dhaniya*)

METHOD

TO BRINE THE CHICKEN:

1. Rinse the whole chicken thoroughly and make deep slits on all sides.
2. In a large bowl, place the chicken and 2½ litres water until the chicken is submerged. Add vinegar and salt and mix well. Soak the chicken in the brine for an hour. Once done, remove the chicken and rinse well.

TO MARINATE THE CHICKEN:

3. In a large bowl, combine all the ingredients for the marinade.
4. Rub the marinade onto the chicken. Fill the marinade into the slits and tie the legs of the chicken together with a thread. Save the remaining marinade.
5. In a broad pan over medium heat, add 2-3 Tbsp of oil and roast the whole chicken. Cook each side for about 5-7 minutes until the chicken is well roasted.

Continued

TO MAKE THE GRAVY:

6. In a blender jar, add all the ingredients for the dried fruit paste with 1 Tbsp water and blend over medium setting to make a thick paste. Set aside.
7. Heat the oil in a wok over medium heat. Add the cinnamon and onions and sauté until the onions are lightly browned.
8. Add the ginger-garlic paste and cook for 1-2 minutes. Add the red chilli pepper powder, salt, garam masala, coriander powder, and roasted cumin seeds.
9. Pour in the remaining marinade and stir well.
10. Add the tomato paste and cook until the excess tomato water dries out and the gravy thickens.
11. Pour in the yoghurt and cook until the oil separates and rises to the surface.
12. Now add the prepared dried fruit paste and saffron, and stir well. Add the chopped coriander and cook for 3-4 minutes.
13. In a another wok over medium heat, add the roasted chicken. Pour over half the gravy over the chicken. Add one cup of water and bring to a boil and simmer for 10 minutes.
14. Cover the wok with a lid and cook one side for 7-8 minutes over low heat.
15. Remove the lid and flip the chicken. Pour the remaining gravy over it. Add another cup of water and boil for 10 minutes. Cover with a lid and cook this side of the chicken for 7-8 minutes over low heat. Once the chicken is cooked and tender, remove from heat.
16. To serve, pour the gravy into a large serving bowl. Set the whole chicken over it. Remove the thread holding its legs together and serve hot with sesame naan (p. 155).

COOKING TIME: **120 MINUTES**

SERVES: **5-6**

MASALA BOTI

Spiced, tender meat chunks in a thick gravy

INGREDIENTS

800 g boneless mutton/lamb, cut into small pieces

1 cup yoghurt (*dahi*)

¼ cup chopped fresh coriander (*dhaniya*)

½ cup chopped fresh mint (*pudina*) leaves

2-4 green chillies (*hari mirch*), finely chopped

½ tsp turmeric (*haldi*) powder

1 tsp coriander (*dhaniya*) powder

1½ tsp red chilli (*lal mirch*) powder

1 tsp wild melon (*kachri*) powder

1 piece of mace (*javetri*), crushed

1 tsp cumin (*jeera*) powder, roasted

1 Tbsp lemon juice

1 tsp garam masala (p. 16)

1 tsp ginger-garlic paste (p. 21)

2 medium-sized onions, browned and crushed

Salt, to taste

120 ml refined oil

Fresh coriander, chopped

COOKING TIME: **60 MINUTES**

METHOD

1. In a large mixing bowl, add the lamb and combine well with yoghurt, coriander, mint leaves, green chillies, turmeric, coriander powder, red chilli powder, wild melon powder, crushed mace, cumin powder, lemon juice, garam masala, ginger-garlic paste, onions, and salt. Let the meat marinate for at least 2-3 hours.
2. In a heavy-bottomed pan over medium heat, add the oil and once it sizzles, pour in the marinated meat along with any residual marinade. Also add half a cup of water.
3. Cover the pan with a lid and bring the gravy to a boil. Reduce the heat after 2-3 minutes.
4. Simmer the meat for 35-40 minutes over low heat until the meat is tender. Be sure to check the cooking progress and stir occasionally.
5. Remove the lid and increase the heat to high to reduce any excess water, allowing the masala to coat the meat evenly.
6. Once the dish has thickened, remove the pan from heat. Garnish with fresh coriander and serve hot with roomali rotis (p. 157).

SERVES: **6-8**

SAAG GOSHT

Tender meat in spicy spinach curry

INGREDIENTS

3 Tbsp refined oil

2 large onions, sliced

1 kg bone-in mutton/lamb (cut into 14-16 pieces)

2 Tbsp ginger-garlic paste (p. 21)

Salt, to taste

1 tsp turmeric (*haldi*) powder

1 tsp red chilli (*lal mirch*) powder

1 tsp coriander (*dhaniya*) powder

3 medium-sized tomatoes, chopped

1½ kg spinach (*palak*), washed and chopped

1 Tbsp dried fenugreek (*kasoori methi*) leaves

6 green chillies, chopped

50 g fresh coriander (*dhaniya*), chopped

1 Tbsp garam masala (p. 16)

METHOD

1. Heat the oil in a pressure cooker over high heat for 2-3 minutes. Reduce the heat to medium, and add the sliced onions. Sauté until they turn pink.
2. Add the lamb, ginger-garlic paste, and season to taste with salt. Stir well.
3. Turn up the heat to high, and add turmeric, red chilli powder, coriander powder, and tomatoes; mix well.
4. Once the tomatoes soften, add the spinach and dried fenugreek leaves, and lock the lid in place.
5. Cook for 3-4 whistles. This will take around 15 minutes. Remove from heat.
6. Let the pressure release and open the lid. Now return the cooker over high heat and simmer for 10 minutes or more. As the oil separates, the meat will become tender and most of the liquid dry out.
7. Remove from heat, add the green chillies, coriander and garam masala. Mix well. Cover and let it rest for a few minutes.
8. Serve hot with tandoori rotis (p. 156).

COOKING TIME: **90 MINUTES**

SERVES: **6-8**

KALI UARD DAL GOSHT

Rich meaty stew with black gram lentils

INGREDIENTS

WHOLE SPICES:

1 cinnamon (*dal chini*) stick

1 star anise (*chakri ke phool*)

2 bay leaves (*tej patta*)

1 black cardamom (*moti elaichi*) pod

100 ml refined oil

1 tomato, chopped

1 Tbsp cumin seeds (*jeera sabut*), roasted

1 large onion, chopped

1 kg bone-in mutton/lamb (cut into 14-16 pieces)

2 Tbsp ginger-garlic paste (p. 21)

Salt, to taste

1 tsp turmeric (*haldi*) powder

1 tsp red chilli (*lal mirch*) powder

1 tsp coriander (*dhaniya*) powder

200 g black gram lentils (*uard dal*), boiled

1 tsp garam masala (p. 16)

1 lemon, juiced

50 g fresh coriander (*dhaniya*), chopped

6 green chillies (*hari mirch*), chopped

1 tsp chaat masala (p. 17)

METHOD

1. In a mixer-grinder, grind the cinnamon, star anise. bay leaves and black cardamom at medium setting for 2-3 minutes until finely powdered. Set aside.
2. In a pan over high heat, add 2 tsp oil. After 2-3 minutes, reduce the heat to medium, and add chopped tomatoes and sauté them for 2-3 minutes. Set aside.
3. Heat the remaining oil in a pressure cooker over high heat for 2-3 minutes. Add the roasted cumin seeds, reduce the heat to medium and add the chopped onions. Sauté until the onions turn light pink.
4. Add the lamb, ginger-garlic paste, and season to taste with salt. Mix well.
5. Add the turmeric, red chilli powder, and coriander powder. Now add the prepared whole spices powder and stir well. Cook for 2 minutes.
6. Stir in the sautéd tomatoes and close the lid of the pressure cooker. Cook for 15 minutes over high heat for 3-4 whistles. Remove from heat and let the pressure release.
7. Open the lid and return the cooker over medium heat. Simmer for 15-20 minutes or until the oil separates.
8. Now add 2 cups of water and bring to a boil.
9. Stir in the boiled dal and simmer for 10 minutes, stirring frequently until the water dries out.
10. Remove from heat and garnish with lemon, fresh coriander, green chilli, and chaat masala. Serve hot with tandoori rotis (p. 156).

COOKING TIME: **90 MINUTES**

SERVES: **6-8**

LAUKI GOSHT

Mutton curry with bottle gourd

INGREDIENTS

150 ml refined oil

1 tomato, chopped

1 large onion, sliced

1 kg bone-in mutton/lamb (cut into 14-16 pieces)

2 Tbsp ginger-garlic paste (p. 21)

Salt, to taste

1 tsp turmeric (*haldi*) powder

1 tsp red chilli (*lal mirch*) powder

1 tsp coriander (*dhaniya*) powder

1 tsp garam masala (p. 16)

2 Tbsp yoghurt (*dahi*)

1 kg bottle gourd (*lauki*), peeled and cubed

50 g fresh coriander (*dhaniya*), chopped

1 tsp chaat masala (p. 17)

4-5 green chillies (*hari mirch*), chopped

METHOD

1. In a pan over high heat, add 2 tsp oil. After 2-3 minutes, reduce the heat to medium and add the chopped tomato. Roast well for 2-3 minutes and remove from heat.
2. In a pressure cooker over high heat, add the remaining oil and wait until it starts to smoke. Reduce the heat to medium and add the sliced onion and sauté until pink.
3. Add the lamb, ginger-garlic paste, and season to taste with salt. Stir well and add the turmeric, red chilli powder, coriander powder, and garam masala. Mix well to combine and cook for 1 minute.
4. Now add the roasted tomatoes (step 1) and lock the lid in place. Cook for 12 minutes over high heat for 3-4 whistles. Remove from heat.
5. Let the pressure release and remove the lid.
6. Return the cooker over high heat and stir in yoghurt. Cook for 10 minutes, stirring frequently.
7. Add the bottle gourd and 1 cup water. Lock the lid and pressure cook again for 10 minutes for 2 whistles, making sure the gourd is well-cooked.
8. Let the pressure release and remove the lid.
9. Now return the cooker to medium heat and cook until the meat becomes tender.
10. Remove from heat and cover before serving to allow the flavours to set in. Garnish with coriander, chaat masala, and green chillies. Serve hot with tandoori rotis (p. 156).

COOKING TIME: **90 MINUTES**

SERVES: **6-8**

TAAR GOSHT

Rampuri delicacy of mutton in a rich yet thin gravy

INGREDIENTS

1 tsp cumin seeds (*jeera*)

300 ml refined oil

7 medium-sized onions, sliced

200 g desi ghee

1 kg bone-in mutton/lamb (cut into 14-16 pieces)

2 Tbsp ginger-garlic paste (p. 21)

100 g korma masala

1 tsp turmeric (*haldi*) powder

1 tsp red chilli pepper (*degi mirch*) powder

1 tsp coriander (*dhaniya*) powder

1 tsp yellow chilli (*peeli mirch*) powder

Salt, to taste

250 g yoghurt (*dahi*)

3 cups water

1 tsp garam masala (p. 16)

METHOD

1. In a small fry pan, dry roast the cumin seeds over high heat for 2-3 minutes until aromatic. Transfer to a small bowl and set aside.
2. In another pan, heat the oil over high heat for 2 minutes. Add 2 onions and deep fry for 5-7 minutes until the onions are crisp and golden brown. Use a slotted spoon to remove and drain on kitchen towels. Once the fried onions are cool, grind them using a mortar and pestle or a blender to make a course paste. Set aside.
3. Heat the ghee in a pressure cooker over high heat for 2-3 minutes. Reduce the heat to medium and add the roasted cumin seeds.
4. Add the remaining sliced onions, lamb, ginger-garlic paste, korma masala, turmeric, red chilli pepper powder, coriander powder, yellow chilli powder, and season to taste with salt. Stir well.
5. Lock the lid in place and cook for 10 minutes over high heat for 3-4 whistles.
6. Let the pressure release and remove the lid.
7. Return the cooker over medium heat. Now add the ground onions and yoghurt. Stir well and simmer for 8-10 minutes, allowing the flavours to meld.
8. Pour in 3 cups of water and lock the lid of the pressure cooker. Cook for 10 minutes over high heat for 3-4 whistles.
9. Check the tenderness of the meat when the pressure is released. If needed, simmer until the meat is fork-tender and cooked to perfection.
10. Remove from heat, add the garam masala and stir. Cover before serving to allow the flavours to set in. Serve hot with tandoori rotis (p. 156).

COOKING TIME: **90 MINUTES**

SERVES: **6-8**

ALOO KEEMA

Minced meat curry with potatoes

INGREDIENTS

WHOLE SPICES:

1 small cinnamon (*dal chini*) stick

2-3 green cardamom (*hari elaichi*) pods

1-2 black cardamom (*moti elaichi*) pods

2-3 bay leaves (*tej patta*)

3-4 cloves (*laung*)

150 ml refined oil

2 medium-sized onions, sliced

1 kg minced mutton/lamb (*keema*), hand-cut

2 medium-sized tomatoes, chopped

2 Tbsp ginger-garlic paste (p. 21)

Salt, to taste

250 g yoghurt (*dahi*)

5-6 medium-sized potatoes, peeled and cubed

3-4 green chillies (*hari mirch*), julienned

Fresh coriander (*dhaniya*), chopped, to garnish

METHOD

1. In a mixer-grinder, blend the whole spices at medium setting for 2-3 minutes until finely powdered.
2. In a pressure cooker over high heat, heat the oil for 2-3 minutes. Reduce the heat to medium and add onions. Sauté until they turn pink.
3. Add the minced lamb, tomatoes, ginger-garlic paste, powdered whole spices, and season to taste with salt. Now reduce the heat to low and lock the lid in place. Cook for 8 minutes, or 3-4 whistles.
4. Let the pressure release and remove the lid.
5. Return the cooker over medium heat and add the yoghurt. Make sure you stir it well to combine. Let simmer for 10 minutes.
6. Add the potatoes, green chillies, 1-2 cups of water and close the lid. Pressure cook again for 5-7 minutes over high heat for 2-3 whistles.
7. Let the pressure release and remove the lid of the cooker. The keema should be tender and cooked well.
8. Garnish with fresh coriander and serve hot with tandoori rotis (p. 156).

COOKING TIME: **70 MINUTES**

SERVES: **6-8**

NARGISI KOFTA

Minced meatballs stuffed with eggs in a rich gravy

INGREDIENTS

WHOLE SPICES:

1 cinnamon (*dal chini*) stick

2 star anise (*chakri ke phool*)

4 green cardamom (*hari elaichi*) pods

4 bay leaves (*tej patta*)

6 cloves (*laung*)

FOR THE MARINADE:

1 kg minced mutton/lamb (*keema*), machine ground

1 large onion, chopped

3-4 green chillies (*hari mirch*), chopped

5 g fresh coriander (*dhaniya*), chopped

1 Tbsp ginger, chopped

2 eggs, whisked

2 Tbsp gram flour (*besan*), roasted

½ tsp turmeric (*haldi*) powder

1 tsp garam masala (p. 16)

1 tsp chaat masala (p. 17)

Salt, to taste

2 Tbsp dried fenugreek (*kasoori methi*) leaves

FOR THE GRAVY:

600 ml refined oil

3 medium-sized onions, pureed

2 medium-sized tomatoes, pureed (p. 22)

2 Tbsp ginger-garlic paste (p. 21)

1 Tbsp red chilli pepper (*degi mirch*) powder

1 Tbsp coriander (*dhaniya*) powder

½ Tbsp turmeric (*haldi*) powder

2 Tbsp yoghurt (*dahi*)

4 eggs, hard-boiled

METHOD

1. In a mixer-grinder, blend the whole spices over medium setting for 2-3 minutes until finely powdered and set aside.
2. In a large bowl, marinate the keema with chopped onion, green chillies, coriander, ginger, whisked eggs, besan, turmeric, garam masala, chaat masala, salt, and dried fenugreek leaves. Combine gently by hand and set aside for 1 hour.
3. Add 200 ml oil to a wok over medium heat. Add the onion puree and cook until brown.
4. Now add the tomato puree, ginger-garlic paste, powdered whole spices, red chilli pepper powder, coriander powder, turmeric and yoghurt. Cook until the oil separates. Now remove from heat and transfer the curry into a large bowl.
5. Divide the marinated keema mixture into 4 portions. Coat the hard-boiled eggs completely with the keema and hand roll each into patties.
6. In a separate wok over high heat, add 400 ml refined oil and deep fry the minced meatball patties until golden brown on all sides. Use a slotted spoon and remove from oil to drain on kitchen towels.
7. Add the patties into the curry bowl, garnish with coriander and serve hot with tandoori rotis (p. 156).

COOKING TIME: **60 MINUTES**

SERVES: **6-8**

SAAG KOFTA

Tender spinach meatballs in a rich gravy

INGREDIENTS

1 ltr water

500 g spinach (*palak*), washed

30 ml mustard oil

2 medium-sized onions, chopped

2 medium-sized tomatoes, chopped

2 Tbsp ginger-garlic paste (p. 21)

Salt, to taste

1 tsp turmeric (*haldi*) powder

1 tsp red chilli (*lal mirch*) powder

1 tsp coriander (*dhaniya*) powder

1 tsp yoghurt (*dahi*)

500 g minced mutton/lamb (*keema*), machine ground

4-5 green chillies, slit and halved

50 g fresh coriander (*dhaniya*)

1 tsp garam masala (p. 16)

1 egg, whisked

METHOD

1. In a cooking pot over high heat, pour 1 litre water and bring to a boil. Add the spinach and boil for 5-6 minutes until the spinach leaves become tender. Remove from heat and set aside. Once cool, drain the leaves and in a mixer-grinder blend them to a smooth puree. Set aside.
2. Heat the oil in a wok over high heat. Reduce the heat to medium as it smokes and add 1 chopped onion and sauté until light pink.
3. Add the tomatoes, ginger-garlic paste, and season to taste with salt. Mix well.
4. Add the turmeric, red chilli powder, coriander powder, spinach puree, and yoghurt. Stir well and simmer for 5-7 minutes. Set the curry aside.
5. In a large bowl, combine the keema with the remaining onion, green chillies, about half fresh coriander, garam masala, whisked egg, and season to taste with salt. Blend together with your fingers to make a soft dough.
6. As the dough sets in a few minutes, wet your hands and shape the keema mixture into equal-sized round portions of a size of your choosing.
7. In a separate pan over medium heat, add 2 cups of water and bring to a boil.
8. Add the keema meatballs into the boiling water and cook for 15-20 minutes until they are cooked through. Use a slotted spoon and remove the meatballs.
9. Place the spinach curry wok back over medium heat and add the meatballs to it, one by one. Gently stir and simmer the curry for 5 minutes.
10. Remove from heat and garnish with the remaining fresh coriander, and serve hot with tandoori rotis (p. 156).

COOKING TIME: **60 MINUTES**

SERVES: **6-8**

PAYA

Slow cooked stew of trotters

INGREDIENTS

200 ml refined oil

3 medium-sized onions, sliced

1 kg mutton/lamb trotters (*paya*)

6 medium-sized tomatoes, peeled and chopped

2 Tbsp ginger-garlic paste (p. 21)

1 tsp turmeric (*haldi*) powder

1 Tbsp red chilli powder (*degi mirch*)

1 tsp coriander (d*haniya*) powder

1 tsp garam masala (p. 16)

1 tsp cumin seeds (*jeera*), roasted

2 bay leaves (*tej patta*)

2 star anise (*chakri ke phool*)

4 green cardamom (*hari elaichi*) pods

1 cinnamon (*dal chini*) stick

4 cloves (*laung*)

Salt, to taste

100 g yoghurt (*dahi*)

METHOD

1. Heat the oil in a pressure cooker over medium heat for 2-3 minutes. Add the onions and sauté until they are soft and translucent.
2. Add the lamb trotters and stir well. Add the tomatoes and ginger-garlic paste. Cook for 2 minutes.
3. Add the turmeric, red chilli powder, coriander powder, and garam masala. Stir well to combine.
4. Add the cumin seeds, bay leaves, star anise, green cardamom, cinnamon, cloves, and season to taste with salt.
5. Now add 2 cups of water and lock the lid in place. Reduce the heat and cook for 3-4 whistles.
6. Let the pressure release and remove the lid. Return the cooker over medium heat and add the yoghurt. Stir well to combine and simmer for 10 minutes.
7. Add 5-6 cups of water and lock the lid to pressure cook for 2-3 whistles. This should take 10-12 minutes.
8. Let the pressure release and open the lid. Stir well and serve hot with tandoori rotis (p. 156).

COOKING TIME: **90 MINUTES**

SERVES: **6-8**

KALEJI

Flavourful lamb liver

INGREDIENTS

WHOLE SPICES:

2 bay leaves (*tej patta*)

4 green cardamom (green *elaichi*) pods

2 1-inch cinnamon (*dal chini*) sticks

4 cloves (*laung*)

1 kg mutton/lamb liver

2 Tbsp ginger-garlic paste (p. 21)

Salt, to taste

1 Tbsp vinegar

200 ml mustard oil

3 medium-sized onions, chopped

1 large tomato, roasted, peeled, and roughly chopped

1 tsp Kashmiri red chilli (*lal mirch*) powder

1 tsp turmeric (*haldi*) powder

1 tsp coriander (*dhaniya*) powder

150 g yoghurt (*dahi*)

1 tsp chaat masala (p. 17)

1 tsp garam masala (p. 16)

1 lemon, juiced

50 g dried fenugreek leaves (*kasoori methi*)

Fresh coriander (*dhaniya*), to garnish

METHOD

1. In a mixer-grinder, blend the whole spices at medium setting for 2-3 minutes until finely ground. Set aside.
2. Rinse the meat thoroughly with cold water.
3. In a large bowl or pot, combine 1 Tbsp ginger-garlic paste, 1 tsp salt, and vinegar in ½ litre water and marinate the meat for 30 minutes.
4. After 30 minutes, rinse thoroughly (about 2-3 times) in fresh water and set aside.
5. In a wok over high heat, add the oil and heat for 2-3 minutes. Reduce the heat to medium and add onions. Sauté until they turn light pink.
6. Add the roasted tomatoes, the remaining ginger-garlic paste, and meat.
7. Add the Kashmiri red chilli powder, turmeric, coriander powder and stir well to combine.
8. Add the prepared ground spices and season to taste with salt. Mix well and cook for a few minutes.
9. Transfer the contents of the wok into a pressure cooker over high heat. Add ½ cup water and 2 tsp salt. Lock the lid in place and cook for 15 minutes, or 3-4 whistles.
10. Let the pressure release and remove the lid.
11. Return the cooker over medium heat and add yoghurt. Stir the yoghurt well and simmer for 8-10 minutes.
12. Reduce the heat; add the chaat masala, garam masala, lemon juice, and dried fenugreek leaves. Cook for 2 minutes or until the preparation dries up.
13. Transfer the dish into a serving bowl and garnish with fresh coriander. Serve hot with roomali rotis (p. 157).

COOKING TIME: **60 MINUTES**

SERVES: **6-8**

SHAB DEG

Slow-cooked turnip and mutton stew

INGREDIENTS

1 kg mutton/lamb (*gole gotti* pieces)

200 ml mustard oil

2 medium-sized onions, sliced

2-3 medium-sized tomatoes, roasted, peeled, and roughly mashed

2 Tbsp ginger-garlic paste (p. 21)

1 tsp red chilli (*lal mirch*) powder

1 tsp turmeric (*haldi*) powder

1 tsp garam masala (p. 16)

1 tsp coriander (*dhaniya*) powder

Salt, to taste

2 Tbsp yoghurt (*dahi*)

750 g turnips (*shuljum*)*

6-8 green chillies (*hari mirch*), chopped

100 g fresh coriander (*dhaniya*), chopped

*The turnips can be substituted with cauliflower to make *Gobhi Gosht*, using the same recipe.

METHOD

1. Rinse the meat thoroughly in cold water.
2. Heat the oil in a pressure cooker over high heat for 2-3 minutes. Reduce the heat to medium and add the onions. Sauté until they turn light pink.
3. Add the meat, tomatoes, and ginger-garlic paste. Sauté for a few minutes.
4. Add the red chilli powder, turmeric, garam masala, coriander powder, and season to taste with salt. Stir well to combine all the ingredients.
5. Add ½ cup water and lock the lid in place. Cook for 8-10 minutes, for 3-4 whistles.
6. Remove from heat and let the pressure release.
7. Return the cooker over medium heat and stir in the yoghurt. Simmer for 10 minutes, stirring occasionally, until the oil separates.
8. Now add the turnips and lock the lid again. Increase the heat to high and pressure cook for 2 whistles. This should take 5 to 6 minutes.
9. Remove from heat and let the pressure release.
10. Transfer the stew into a serving bowl and garnish with green chillies and coriander. Serve hot with tandoori rotis (p. 156).

COOKING TIME: **60 MINUTES**

SERVES: **6-8**

RAAN

Succulent slow-cooked leg of lamb

INGREDIENTS

SPICES:

2 bay leaves (*tej patta*)

4 green cardamom (*hari elaichi*) pods

1 black cardamom (*moti elaichi*) pod

6 cloves (*laung*)

1 nutmeg (*jaiphal*)

½ mace (*javitri*)

1 tsp cumin seeds (*jeera*)

1 tsp coriander seeds (*dhaniya*)

1 tsp fennel seeds (*saunf*)

1 kg leg of mutton/lamb (*raan*)

100 ml refined oil

200 g yoghurt (*dahi*)

1 Tbsp vinegar

2 Tbsp raw papaya (*kaccha papita*) paste

1 cup whole wheat flour, to seal the pan

1 lemon, cut into wedges

1 tsp chaat masala (p. 17)

METHOD

1. In a fry pan over medium heat, add all the whole spices and dry roast them for 2-3 minutes. Once cool, add them to a mortar and pestle or mixer-grinder and grind them to a fine powder.
2. Rinse the lamb leg thoroughly and let it dry over kitchen towel. Pound it with a heavy object to flatten it.
3. In a mixing bowl, marinate the meat with oil, yoghurt, vinegar, raw papaya, and ground spices. Leave overnight or for 8 hours in the refrigerator.
4. In another bowl, take the wheat flour and water as needed and knead into a tight dough. Set aside.
5. When ready to cook the meat, take a large pan or wok that can comfortably fit the meat. Transfer the marinated meat into the pan.
6. Cover the pan with a lid and seal with the dough ensuring the vessel is covered and tightly sealed on the edges.
7. Now place the dough-sealed pan or wok over low heat and cook for 2 hours.
8. Open the seal after 2 hours and let the dish simmer until the curry is of the desired consistency.
9. Remove from heat and slice the meat into preferred sizes. Garnish with lemon wedges and chaat masala. Serve hot with sheermal (p. 161).

COOKING TIME: **2 HOURS**

SERVES: **4-6**

BHUNA GOSHT

Roasted mutton curry

INGREDIENTS

150 ml refined oil or desi ghee

3 medium-sized onions, sliced

1 kg bone-in mutton/lamb

2 Tbsp ginger-garlic paste (p. 21)

3 medium-sized tomatoes, roasted, peeled, and roughly chopped

Salt, to taste

1 tsp turmeric (*haldi*) powder

1 tsp coriander (*dhaniya*) powder

1 tsp red chilli (*lal mirch*) powder

1 tsp garam masala (p. 16)

WHOLE SPICES:

1 star anise (*chakri ke phool*)

1 green cardamom (*hari elaichi*) pod

2 bay leaves (*tej patta*)

2 1-inch cinnamon (*dal chini*) sticks

4 cloves (*laung*)

100 g yoghurt (*dahi*)

6-8 green chillies, chopped

50 g fresh coriander (*dhaniya*), chopped

50 g meat masala (store-bought)

Small piece ginger, julienned

METHOD

1. Heat the oil/ghee in a pressure cooker over high heat for 2-3 minutes. Add the onions and sauté until they are light pink.
2. Add the mutton pieces, ginger-garlic paste, tomatoes, and season to taste with salt. Combine well and sauté for 2 minutes.
3. Add the turmeric, coriander powder, red chilli powder, and garam masala. Stir well to combine.
4. In a small muslin bag add the whole spices. Tie it securely with a kitchen twine and place it in the pressure cooker.
5. Pour in half a cup of water and lock the lid. Cook for 3-4 whistles. This should take around 8-10 minutes.
6. Remove from heat and let the pressure release. Open the lid and add the yoghurt. Stirring frequently, now roast the meat for 7-8 minutes.
7. Add the green chillies, fresh coriander, and meat masala, and lock the lid again.
8. Reduce the heat to low and cook for 3-4 whistles.
9. Remove from heat and let the pressure release. Check the meat for tenderness.
10. Use a slotted spoon to remove the spice potli and serve hot with tandoori rotis (p. 156).

COOKING TIME: **90 MINUTES**

SERVES: **6-8**

KARELA KEEMA

Spicy curry made with bitter gourd and minced meat

INGREDIENTS

1 kg bitter gourds (*karela*)

Salt, to taste

A pinch of calcium carbonate (*choona*)

3 Tbsp mustard oil

1 cup refined oil

1 tsp cumin seeds (*jeera sabut*)

2 large onions, sliced

1 kg minced mutton/lamb (*keema*), hand-cut

1 tomato, roasted, peeled, and chopped

2 Tbsp ginger-garlic paste (p. 21)

1 tsp red chilli pepper (*degi mirch*) powder

1 tsp Kashmiri red chilli (*lal mirch*) powder

1 tsp coriander (*dhaniya*) powder

WHOLE SPICES:

1 star anise (*chakri ke phool*)

2 green cardamom (*hari elaichi*) pods

1 bay leaf (*tej patta*)

1-inch cinnamon (*dal chini*) stick

50 g yoghurt (*dahi*)

6-8 green chillies (*hari mirch*), finely chopped

1 tsp garam masala (p. 16)

1 tsp chaat masala (p. 17)

50 g fresh coriander (*dhaniya*), chopped

COOKING TIME: **90 MINUTES**

METHOD

1. Peel and slit the bitter gourds and slice them into small pieces.
2. In a cooking pot over medium heat, add 2 litres water, 1 Tbsp salt, and a pinch of calcium carbonate and bring to a boil. Add the bitter gourds and cook for 20 minutes.
3. Remove from heat and drain. Repeat the boiling process with fresh water, salt, and calcium carbonate. Remove from heat and let cool. Squeeze out any excess water by hand and spread the gourds over a muslin cloth to dry.
4. Heat the oil in a skillet over medium heat. Add the bitter gourds and sauté for 2-3 minutes until they turn pale yellow. Use a slotted spoon and drain on kitchen towels.
5. In a pressure cooker over medium heat, add the oil and heat for 2-3 minutes. Add the cumin seeds and once they splutter, add the onions, minced meat, tomatoes, and ginger-garlic paste. Stir well.
6. Add the red chilli pepper powder, Kashmiri chilli powder, and coriander powder.
7. Add the whole spices to a muslin bag and tie the bag securely with a kitchen twine. Place the spice bag into the pressure cooker.
8. Add 1 cup water and lock the lid in place. Cook for 3-4 whistles (10 to 12 minutes).
9. Remove from heat and let the pressure release. Open the lid and return the cooker to medium heat. Now add the yoghurt, green chillies, garam masala, chaat masala and simmer until excess water evaporates.
10. Add the fried gourds and half a cup of water. Lock the lid again and cook for 3-4 whistles.
11. Remove from heat and let the pressure release. Discard the spice bag and garnish with fresh coriander.

SERVES: **6-6**

BHARVA KARELA KEEMA

Bitter gourd stuffed with minced meat

INGREDIENTS

1 kg bitter gourds (*karela*)

Salt, to taste

100 ml mustard oil

1 medium-sized onion, finely chopped

1 medium-sized tomato, roasted, peeled, and chopped

½ kg minced mutton/lamb (*keema*)

1 Tbsp ginger-garlic paste (p. 21)

1 tsp red chilli pepper (*degi mirch*) powder

1 tsp coriander (*dhaniya*) powder

1 tsp turmeric (*haldi*) powder

1 Tbsp yoghurt (*dahi*)

½ Tbsp garam masala (p. 16)

1 tsp chaat masala (p. 17)

1 tsp cumin (*jeera*) powder

4-6 green chillies (*hari mirch*), chopped

50 g fresh coriander (dhaniya), chopped

METHOD

1. Rinse the bitter gourds with fresh water and wipe them dry with a clean kitchen towel. Peel the gourds and make a cut on each vertically, keeping the base intact. Remove the seeds with a spoon.
2. In a cooking pot over medium heat, add 2 litres water with 1 Tbsp salt and bring to a boil. Add the gourds to the pot and cook for 20 minutes. Remove from heat and drain excess water. Repeat the process with fresh water to double-boil without adding salt. Once done, drain and spread them over a muslin cloth to dry.
3. In a pressure cooker over high heat, add half the oil. Once it begins to simmer, add the onions and sauté until brown.
4. Add the tomatoes and cook until they are tender.
5. Add the minced meat, ginger-garlic paste, red chilli pepper powder, coriander powder, and turmeric. Lock the lid in place and cook for 3-4 whistles. This should take around 10 to 12 minutes.
6. Remove the cooker from heat and let the pressure release. Open the lid and return the cooker over medium heat. Stir in the yoghurt and continue cooking until the meat dries out.
7. Add the garam masala, chaat masala, cumin powder, green chillies, and fresh coriander. Stir well to combine.
8. Remove from heat and set aside to cool.
9. Once cool, stuff the prepared keema masala into the gourds and secure each with a thick kitchen thread.
10. In a wok over medium heat, heat the remaining oil and shallow fry the bitter gourds until they turn golden brown.
11. Remove the threads and serve on a flat serving dish with chappatis (p. 154).

COOKING TIME: **90 MINUTES**

SERVES: **4-6**

PASANDE MUTTON

Tender boneless meat cooked in a rich, spicy gravy

INGREDIENTS

200 g ghee

1 tsp cumin seeds (*jeera sabut*)

4 dry red chillies (*sookhi sabut lal mirch*)

4 large onions, chopped

1 kg *pasande* mutton/lamb, boneless

2 Tbsp ginger-garlic paste

WHOLE SPICES:

2 star anise (*chakri ke phool*)

2 green cardamom (*hari elaichi*) pods

1 black cardamom (*moti elaichi*) pod

2 bay leaves (*tej patta*)

1-inch cinnamon (*dal chini*) stick

4 cloves (*laung*)

1 tsp red chilli (*lal mirch*) powder

100 g yoghurt (*dahi*)

6 green chillies (*hari mirch*), chopped

1 tsp garam masala (p. 16)

½ lemon, juiced

1 tsp chaat masala (p. 17)

Salt, to taste

METHOD

1. In a pressure cooker over medium heat, add the ghee and heat for 2-3 minutes.
2. Add the cumin seeds and dry red chillies, and roast until they splutter. Add the onions and sauté until they are light pink.
3. Add the lamb and ginger-garlic paste; stir well and sauté for 2 to 3 minutes.
4. In a small muslin bag add all the whole spices and tie the bag securely with a kitchen twine. Drop it into the pressure cooker and pour 1 cup water.
5. Lock the lid in place. Increase the heat to high and cook for 3-4 whistles. This should take around 8 to 10 minutes.
6. Remove from heat and let the pressure release.
7. Open the lid and return the cooker over medium heat. Let the gravy simmer until the excess water evaporates.
8. Add the red chilli powder, yoghurt, green chillies, garam masala, lemon juice, chaat masala and stir well. Season to taste with salt.
9. Cover the cooker with a flat plate or lid and cook for 2-3 minutes to allow the flavours to combine.
10. Remove from heat and discard the bag of whole spices. Serve hot with roomali rotis (p. 157).

COOKING TIME: **75 MINUTES**

SERVES: **6-8**

KHATTA GOSHT

Tender meat cooked in a yoghurt curry

INGREDIENTS

1 kg bone-in mutton/lamb, cut into 14-16 pieces

3 large onions, sliced

1 Tbsp ginger-garlic paste (p. 21)

250 g ghee

400 g yoghurt (*dahi*)

4 green cardamom (*hari elaichi*) pods

2 black cardamom (*moti elaichi*) pods

10 dry red chillies (*sookhi lal mirch*)

1 tsp turmeric (*haldi*) powder

Salt, to taste

METHOD

1. In a large cooking pot, combine all the ingredients: mutton, onions, ginger-garlic paste, ghee, yoghurt, green cardamom, black cardamom, red chillies, and turmeric. Season to taste with salt and mix well using your hands.
2. Place the pot over low heat and cook for 60 minutes, stirring frequently.
3. Now cover the pot with a lid and simmer for another 30 minutes, or until the meat is tender and the oil separates. Stir occassionally.
4. Remove from heat and serve hot with tandoori rotis (p. 156).

COOKING TIME: **90 MINUTES**

SERVES: **6-8**

TAMATAR GOSHT

A tangy meat curry with tomatoes

INGREDIENTS

WHOLE SPICES:

1-inch cinnamon (*dal chini*) stick

1 star anise (*chakri ke phool*)

2 bay leaves (*tej patta*)

150 ml refined oil

3 large onions, sliced

1 kg bone-in mutton/lamb (cut into 14-16 pieces)

2 Tbsp ginger-garlic paste (p. 21)

Salt, to taste

1 tsp turmeric (*haldi*) powder

1 tsp red chilli (*lal mirch*) powder

1 tsp coriander (*dhaniya*) powder

½ kg tomatoes, roasted, peeled, and chopped

2 green chillies (*hari mirch*), chopped

50 g fresh coriander (*dhaniya*), chopped

Small piece ginger, julienned

1 tsp garam masala (p. 16)

METHOD

1. In a mixer-grinder, grind the whole spices at medium setting for 2-3 minutes into a fine powder. Set aside.
2. In a pressure cooker over high heat, heat the oil for 2-3 minutes. Reduce the heat to medium and add the onions. Sauté until they turn light pink.
3. Now add the mutton and ginger-garlic paste. Season to taste with salt and add the turmeric, red chilli powder, and coriander powder. Also add the prepared ground spices. Stir well to combine.
4. Add the tomatoes and lock the lid in place. Cook over high heat for 4-5 whistles. This should take around 12 to 15 minutes.
5. Remove from heat and let the pressure release.
6. Open the lid, and return the cooker over medium heat. Simmer until the excess water evaporates. At this point, the meat should be tender and the oil should have separated. Remove from heat.
7. Add the green chillies, fresh coriander, julienned ginger, and garam masala. Mix well.
8. Cover the dish and leave for a few minutes to allow the flavours to combine well.
9. Serve hot with tandoori rotis (p. 156).

COOKING TIME: **60 MINUTES**

SERVES: **6-8**

MUTTON KEEMA ISHTEW

A comforting, hearty dish in a flavourful broth

INGREDIENTS

WHOLE SPICES:

2 1-inch cinnamon (*dal chini*) sticks

6 green cardamom (green *elaichi*) pods

2 star anise (*chakri ke phool*)

4 black cardamom (*moti elaichi*) pods

6 cloves (*laung*)

1 bay leaf (*tej patta*)

150 ml refined oil

8 onions, sliced

1 tsp cumin seeds (*jeera sabut*)

1 kg minced mutton/lamb (*keema*)

2 Tbsp ginger-garlic paste (p. 21)

Salt, to taste

150 g desi ghee

6 dry whole red chillies (*sookhi sabut lal mirch*)

150 g yoghurt (*dahi*)

1 tsp garam masala (p. 16)

1 tsp chaat masala (p. 17)

6-8 large green chillies (*hari mirch*), chopped

1 lemon, juiced

METHOD

1. In a mixer-grinder, blend the whole spices at medium setting for 2-3 minutes until finely powdered. Set aside.
2. In a pressure cooker over high heat, add the oil and heat for 2-3 minutes. Reduce the heat to medium, and add 2 sliced onions. Sauté until they soften and turn translucent.
3. Add the cumin seeds, keema, ginger-garlic paste and season to taste with salt. Stir well.
4. Lock the lid in place and cook for 3 whistles. Remove from heat and let the pressure release.
5. Separately, in a large wok over medium heat, add the ghee and the remaining onions. Sauté the onions until they turn light pink. Add the red chillies.
6. Remove the lid of the pressure cooker and transfer the keema into the wok. Add the powdered whole spices and stir-fry well.
7. Stir in the yoghurt, garam masala, chaat masala, green chillies, and lemon juice. Cook for 20 minutes, stirring frequently, until the meat is cooked.
8. Remove from heat and cover until serving to allow the flavours to meld.
9. Serve hot with roomali rotis (p. 157).

* The bone-in lamb can be substituted with lamb keema to make *Keema Ishtew*, using the same recipe.

COOKING TIME: **60 MINUTES**

SERVES: **6-8**

MUTTON KORMA

Creamy and spicy meat curry

INGREDIENTS

300 ml oil

5 medium-sized onions, sliced

220 g ghee

150-200 g korma masala (store-bought)

1 Tbsp ginger-garlic paste (p. 21)

2 tsp turmeric (*haldi*) powder

1 tsp red chilli pepper (*degi mirch*) powder

1 tsp Kashmiri red chilli (*lal mirch*) powder

1 tsp coriander (*dhaniya*) powder

1 green cardamom (*hari elaichi*) pod

1 star anise (*chakri ke phool*)

1 bay leaf (*tej patta*)

1 kg bone-in mutton/lamb, cut into 14-16 pieces

400 g yoghurt (*dahi*)

Salt, to taste

4 cups water

1 tsp chaat masala (p. 17)

1 tsp garam masala (p. 16)

METHOD

1. In a heavy-bottomed frying pan over medium heat, add the oil and 2 onions. Fry them until golden brown. Use a slooted spoon and remove to drain on kitchen towels. Once they are cool, add them to a grinder jar and grind to a coarse paste. Set aside.
2. In a pressure cooker over medium heat, add the ghee and let it heat for 2-3 minutes. Add the remaining sliced onions and sauté until they are tender.
3. Add the korma masala, ginger-garlic paste, turmeric, red chilli pepper powder, Kashmiri chilli powder, and coriander powder. Stir well to combine.
4. Add the green cardamom, star anise and bay leaf, and stir.
5. Now add the meat and stir in the yoghurt. Season to taste with salt.
6. Increase the heat to high and lock the lid in place. Cook for 3-4 whistles; this should take around 8 to 10 minutes.
7. Remove from heat and let the pressure release. Open the lid and stir well.
8. Now return the cooker over high heat and add the prepared onion paste. Cook for 10 minutes.
9. Add 4 cups of water and lock the lid of the pressure cooker. Cook for 3-4 whistles. This should take around 10 minutes.
10. Remove from heat and let the pressure release. Open the lid and simmer until the meat is tender.
11. Add the chaat masala, garam masala, and stir to combine well.
12. Remove from heat and cover. Allow it to rest covered for a few minutes before serving hot with tandoori rotis (p. 156).

COOKING TIME: **90 MINUTES**

SERVES: **6-8**

MOTI HARI MIRCH KEEMA

Spicy minced meat cooked with large green chillies

INGREDIENTS

WHOLE SPICES:

1 cinnamon (*dal chini*) stick

4 green cardamom (*hari elaichi*) pods

2 star anise (*chakri ke phool*)

1 bay leaf (*tej patta*)

4 cloves (*laung*)

150 ml mustard oil

3 large onions, sliced

1 kg minced mutton/lamb (*keema*), hand-cut

2 tomatoes, peeled and chopped

2 Tbsp ginger-garlic paste (p. 21)

1 tsp turmeric (*haldi*) powder

1 tsp red chilli pepper (*degi mirch*) powder

1 tsp coriander (*dhaniya*) powder

Salt, to taste

150 g yoghurt (*dahi*)

8-10 large green chilli peppers (*moti hari mirch*)*, chopped

½ cup water

Fresh coriander leaves, chopped

METHOD

1. In a mixer-grinder, grind the whole spices at medium setting for 2-3 minutes until finely powdered. Set aside.
2. In a pressure cooker over high heat, heat the mustard oil for 2-3 minutes. Reduce the heat to medium and add the onions. Sauté until they turn light pink.
3. Add the keema, tomatoes, ginger-garlic paste, turmeric, red chilli pepper powder, coriander powder, powdered whole spices, and season to taste with salt. Stir well to combine.
4. Lock the lid in place and cook for 1 whistle.
5. Reduce the heat to medium and cook for 10 more minutes.
6. Remove from heat and let the pressure release. Open the lid of the pressure cooker and stir in the yoghurt.
7. Return the cooker over medium heat and simmer for about 10 minutes.
8. Add the green chilli peppers and ½ cup water. Let simmer for 10 minutes until the meat and chillies are tender and cooked well.
9. Remove from heat and garnish with fresh coriander. Serve hot with tandoori rotis (p. 156).

*The large green chilli peppers can be substituted with sautéd okra to make *Bhindi Keema*.

COOKING TIME: **60 MINUTES**

SERVES: **6-8**

BHEJA FRY

Spicy mutton brain curry

INGREDIENTS

150 g refined oil

1 large onion, chopped

2 tomatoes, roasted, peeled, and chopped

2 Tbsp ginger-garlic paste (p. 21)

2 tsp turmeric (*haldi*) powder

1 tsp garam masala (p. 16)

1 tsp coriander (*dhaniya*) powder

Salt, to taste

2 pieces of mutton/lamb brain

1 tsp chaat masala (p. 17)

1 lemon, juiced

100 g fresh coriander (*dhaniya*), chopped

4-6 large green chillies (*hari mirch*), chopped

METHOD

1. Heat the oil in a heavy-bottomed frying pan over medium heat for 2-3 minutes. Add the onions and sauté until they turn light pink.
2. Add the tomatoes, ginger-garlic paste, 1 tsp turmeric, garam masala, and coriander powder. Season to taste with salt and add 2 tablespoon water. Stir and cook for 10 minutes. Remove from heat and set aside.
3. In a pot over medium heat, add ½ litre water and bring to a boil. Now add the brain pieces with 1 tsp turmeric and ½ tsp salt and cook for 10-15 minutes or until done. Remove from heat, drain excess water, and scramble the meat.
4. Add the meat to the frying pan with the curry.
5. Return the frying pan over medium heat and cook until the oil separates, stirring frequently for 5 minutes. Remove from heat.
6. Garnish with chaat masala, lemon juice, fresh coriander, and green chillies. Serve hot with chappatis (p. 154).

COOKING TIME: **45 MINUTES**

SERVES: **2-4**

MUTTON NIHARI

Slow-cooked spicy meat in a thick gravy

INGREDIENTS

1 kg bone-in mutton/lamb, cut into 14-16 pieces

300 ml refined oil

100 g Nihari masala (p. 19) or store bought nihari masala

2 Tbsp ginger-garlic paste (p. 21)

4 large onions, sliced, fried, and ground

4-5 cups water

100 g wheat flour

FOR TEMPERING:

1 tsp ghee

1 (1") piece ginger (*adrak*), julienned

½ tsp red chilli (*lal mirch*) powder

FOR GARNISHING:

2 green chillies (*hari mirch*), chopped

1 (1") piece ginger, julienned

½ lemon, quartered into wedges

2 Tbsp fried onions

METHOD

1. Clean and wash the meat thoroughly.
2. In a large wok over high heat, add the oil and heat for 2-3 minutes.
3. Add the meat and stir in ginger-garlic paste, Nihari masala, and red chilli pepper powder. Cook for 30 minutes, stirring frequently.
4. Add the ground onions and sauté for 5 minutes.
5. Add 4 to 5 cups water and bring to a boil.
6. Now add the wheat flour and stir well. Reduce the heat to low and cover the wok with a lid. Let the nihari simmer for one hour. Keep stirring occasionally.
7. In a separate pan over high heat, make the tempering by heating the ghee. Add the ginger and red chilli powder, and sauté for 5 minutes.
8. Pour the tempering over the nihari and stir well to combine.
9. Now garnish with chopped green chillies, julienned ginger, chopped coriander, and lemon. Top it off with brown onions and serve hot with tandoori rotis (p. 156).

COOKING TIME: **2 HOURS**

SERVES: **4-6**

BHINDI GOSHT

Tender meat with okra

INGREDIENTS

WHOLE SPICES:

1-inch cinnamon (*dal chini*) stick

2-3 green cardamom (*hari elaichi*) pods

2 black cardamom (*moti elaichi*) pods

1 bay leaf (*tej patta*)

300 g okra (*bhindi*)*

2 Tbsp mustard oil

2 large onions, chopped

1 kg bone-in mutton/lamb, cut into 14-16 pieces

2 Tbsp ginger-garlic paste (p. 21)

2 large tomatoes, chopped

1 tsp cumin seeds (*jeera seeds*), roasted

1 tsp coriander (*dhaniya*) powder

1 tsp red chilli (*lal mirch*) powder

1 tsp turmeric (*haldi*) powder

Salt, to taste

2 Tbsp yoghurt (*dahi*)

3-4 green chillies (*hari mirch*), chopped

3 cups water

1 tsp garam masala (p. 16)

METHOD

1. In a mixer-grinder, grind the whole spices (cinnamon, green cardamom, black cardamom, and bay leaf) at medium setting for 2-3 minutes to a fine powder. Set aside.
2. Rinse the okra thoroughly and pat dry on kitchen towels. Chop off the tops and bottom and slit them in halves.
3. In a pressure cooker over high heat, add the oil and heat for 2-3 minutes. Reduce the heat to medium and add the okra and onions. Sauté until the onions turn light pink.
4. Add the mutton and ginger-garlic paste, and sauté for a few minutes, until the raw smell is gone.
5. Add the tomatoes, powdered whole spices, cumin seeds, coriander powder, red chilli powder, turmeric, and season to taste with salt. Stir well and sauté for 2-3 minutes.
6. Lock the lid in place and over high heat, cook for 2-3 whistles. This should take around 6-7 minutes.
7. Remove from heat and let the pressure release.
8. Open the lid and return the cooker over medium heat and simmer for 15 minutes, stirring frequently.
9. Add the yoghurt, green chillies, and 3 cups water.
10. Lock the lid in place and increase the heat to high. Pressure cook for 4-5 whistles. This should take around 10 minutes.
11. Remove from heat and let the pressure release.
12. Open the lid and return the cooker over medium heat. Simmer until the meat is tender. Sprinkle the garam masala and stir well.
13. Remove from heat and cover until serving to allow the flavours to meld together. Serve with tandoori rotis (p. 156).

*Okra can be substituted with potatoes to make *Aloo Gosht* and with taro root to make *Arbi Gosht*.

COOKING TIME: **60 MINUTES**

SERVES: **6-8**

FISH CURRY

Flavourful gravy with tender fish

INGREDIENTS

1 lemon, juiced

1½ Tbsp ginger-garlic paste (p. 31)

1 kg sole fish, chopped

Salt, to taste

1 tsp turmeric (*haldi*) powder

250 ml mustard oil

3 large onions, made to a paste (p. 22)

3 large tomatoes, made to a paste (p. 22)

1 tsp red chilli pepper (*degi mirch*) powder

1 tsp coriander (*dhaniya*) powder

1 tsp red chilli (*lal mirch*) powder

½ tsp garam masala (p. 16)

COOKING TIME: **60 MINUTES**

METHOD

1. In a large bowl, combine the lemon juice and ½ Tbsp ginger-garlic paste. Add the fish and enough water to submerge it completely. Leave the fish to soak in this mixture for 30 minutes.
2. After 30 minutes, rinse the pieces thoroughly until there is no smell remaining. Dry it over a muslin cloth and transfer into a separate large bowl.
3. Season to taste with salt and add ½ tsp turmeric; rub all over the pieces.
4. In a heavy-bottom pan over high heat, add 200 ml mustard oil. When it begins to simmer, reduce the heat to medium, and shallow fry the fish in batches, cooking both sides until golden brown. Use a slotted spoon and drain on kitchen towels. Set aside.

TO MAKE THE GRAVY:

5. Heat the remaining oil in a wok over high heat. When it begins to simmer, add the onion paste and sauté until it browns.
6. Reduce the heat to medium and add the tomato paste, the remaining ginger-garlic paste, ½ tsp turmeric, chilli pepper powder, coriander powder, and red chilli powder. Stir well and cook over high heat until the oil separates.
7. Add 2 cups of water and bring to a boil, stirring continuously. Season to taste with salt.
8. Add the fried fish pieces and garam masala. Reduce the heat to low and simmer for 10 minutes.
9. Remove from heat and cover the wok with a lid until serving. Serve with steamed rice.

SERVES: **4-5**

RICE
&
BREADS

ALOO TEHRI

Fragrant basmati rice with potatoes

INGREDIENTS

500 g basmati rice

120 ml refined oil

1 medium-sized onion, sliced

½ tsp cumin seeds (*jeera sabut*)

1 tsp ginger-garlic paste (p. 21)

1 medium-sized tomato, chopped

4 medium-sized potatoes, sliced lengthwise

½ tsp turmeric (*haldi*) powder

½ tsp red chilli pepper (*degi mirch*) powder

½ tsp dried fenugreek leaves (*kasoori methi*)

4 cups water

Salt, to taste

2-3 green chillies (*hari mirch*), slit lengthwise

METHOD

1. Rinse the rice well for a couple of times until the water runs clear of starch. Soak them in 1 litre water for 30 minutes.
2. In a pot over medium heat, add the oil and heat for 2-3 minutes. Add the onion and cumin seeds. Sauté until the onion turns golden.
3. Add the ginger-garlic paste and tomato. Stir well and cook until the tomatoes soften.
4. Add the potatoes and roast them for 6-8 minutes, stirring frequently.
5. Now add the turmeric, red chilli pepper powder, and dried fenugreek leaves. Cook for 2-3 minutes, adding a splash of water if the spices begin to stick to the bottom.
6. Add 4 cups water and season to taste with salt. As the water begins to boil, add the drained rice and stir well. Cook over medium to high heat until the water has mostly evaporated and the rice is almost done.
7. Once the water evaporates, add the green chillies on top.
8. Cover the pot with a lid and simmer over low heat until the rice is fully cooked. Any excess water should have dried out and the rice should look glossy.
9. Remove from heat and serve hot with mint chutney (p. 23) and yoghurt.

COOKING TIME: **40 MINUTES**

SERVES: **6-8**

MUTTON BIRYANI

Aromatic rice layered with tender meat, spiced to perfection

INGREDIENTS

750 g golden sella rice

Salt, to taste

300 g desi ghee

1 large onion, finely sliced

1 kg bone-in mutton/lamb, chopped into 16-18 pieces

200 g biryani masala (p. 18) or store bought biryani masala

1 Tbsp ginger-garlic paste (p. 21)

250 g yoghurt (*dahi*)

150 g green chilli pickle (store bought of any preferred make)

¼ tsp edible red colour, soaked in 1 Tbsp milk for 2 minutes

METHOD

1. Rinse the rice well for a couple of times until the water runs clear of starch. Now soak them in enough water for 1 hour. Drain gently in a colander.
2. In a cooking pot over high heat, combine the soaked rice with 1½ litres water and bring to a boil.
3. Season to taste with salt and add 100 g ghee. Simmer for 5-7 minutes until the rice is half-cooked. Remove from heat and drain excess water. Set aside.
4. Heat 100 g ghee in a pressure cooker over high heat. Add the onions and sauté until they turn light pink.
5. Add the mutton, biryani masala, ginger-garlic paste, and season to taste with salt. Lock the lid in place and cook for 2-3 whistles. This should take around 8 minutes.
6. Let the pressure release and open the lid.
7. Now return the cooker to medium heat and stir in the yoghurt. Roast the mutton until the water has dried.
8. Layer the lamb with green chilli pickle.
9. Reduce the heat to low and lock the lid of the cooker. Cook for another 2-3 whistles.
10. Remove from heat and let the pressure release. Open the lid and add the edible red colour.
11. Now add the rice and cover the cooker with a flat plate. Cook until the water dries out, stirring occasionally.
12. Add the remaining 100 g ghee and cover until all the flavours have melded together.
13. Remove from heat and serve with a side of raita of choice.

COOKING TIME: **90 MINUTES**

SERVES: **6-8**

YAKHNI PULAO

A delicacy of fragrant rice cooked in spicy meat broth

INGREDIENTS

750 g basmati rice

1 kg bone-in mutton/lamb, cut into 16-18 pieces

Salt, to taste

150 g ghee

1 tsp cumin seeds (*jeera sabut*)

6-8 dry red chillies (*sookhi sabut lal mirch*)

2 medium-sized onions, sliced

1 Tbsp ginger-garlic paste

½ Tbsp ginger, minced

½ Tbsp garlic, minced

WHOLE SPICES:

4 bay leaves (*tej patta*)

6 green cardamom (*hari elaichi*) pods

2 black cardamom (*moti elaichi*) pods

8 cloves (*laung*)

2 cinnamon (*dal chini*) sticks

3 star anise (*chakri ke phool*)

8-10 black peppercorns (*kali mirch*)

200 g yoghurt (*dahi*)

8 green chillies (*hari mirch*), chopped

½ tsp garam masala (p. 16)

FOR TEMPERING:

½ cup oil

COOKING TIME: **90 MINUTES**

METHOD

1. Rinse the rice well for a couple of times until the water runs clear of starch. Soak in 1½ litres water for atleast an hour before cooking. Drain gently.
2. In a pressure cooker over high heat, add 8 cups of water along with the mutton and 1 tsp salt.
3. Add the ghee, cumin seeds, dry red chillies, 1 sliced onion, ginger-garlic paste, and the minced ginger and garlic.
4. Add the whole spices in a muslin potli and tie securely with kitchen twine. Place the potli in the cooker.
5. Lock the lid in place and cook for 1 whistle.
6. Remove from heat and let the pressure release before taking off the lid.
7. Return the cooker over medium heat and stir in the yoghurt. Combine well. Also add the green chillies and simmer for 2-3 minutes. Remove from heat.
8. Sieve the broth into a bowl and remove the whole spices potli. Use a slotted spoon and transfer the lamb into another bowl. Set aside.
9. In a pot over high heat, add the broth, lamb, garam masala, and soaked rice. Season to taste with salt. Reduce the heat and cover the pot with a lid. Cook for 25 minutes until the water dries out completely. Remove from heat.

TO MAKE THE TEMPERING:

10. Heat the oil in a small wok over medium heat. Add the remaining sliced onion and fry until golden brown. Pour over the pulao when done. Serve hot with *dahi phulki* (p. 169) and mint chutney (p. 23).

SERVES: **6-8**

KHICHDA

Hearty mixed-grain stew

INGREDIENTS

DAL MIX:

100 g black lentils (sabut *urad*)
100 g red lentils (*lal masoor*)
100 g brown lentils (sabut *masoor*)
100 g barley (*jow*)
50 g wheat
50 g rice

WHOLE SPICES:

2 bay leaves (*tej patta*)
1 star anise (*chakri ke phool*)
2-3 black cardamom (*moti elaichi*) pods
5-6 green cardamom (*hari elaichi*) pods
5-6 cloves (*laung*)
1-inch cinnamon (*dal chini*) stick

Salt, to taste
½ tsp turmeric (*haldi*) powder
2 tsp ginger-garlic paste (p. 21)
60 g Haleem masala (p. 20)
150 ml refined oil
2 onions, sliced
2 small-sized tomatoes, roasted
1 kg bone-in mutton/ lamb, chopped into 14-16 pieces
100 g yoghurt (*dahi*)
½ tsp red chilli powder

FOR TEMPERING & GARNISHING:

2 Tbsp oil
1 large onion, sliced
2 green chillies (*hari mirch*), chopped
1 (1") piece ginger, julienned
1 lemon, quartered into wedges
2 Tbsp fried onions

COOKING TIME: **90 MINUTES**

METHOD

1. Rinse the dal mix and soak them together in 1 litre water overnight, or for 8 hours.
2. In a small pan over medium heat, dry roast all the whole spices and grind to a fine powder.
3. In a pressure cooker over medium heat, add the soaked dal mix, 8 cups of water, ½ tsp salt, turmeric, 1 tsp ginger-garlic paste, and 30 g Haleem masala. Reduce the heat and lock the lid in place. Cook for 1 whistle.
4. Remove from heat and let the pressure release. Open the lid and return the cooker over medium heat. Simmer for 30-35 minutes until the excess water dries out. Remove from heat and set aside.
5. In a separate pressure cooker over medium heat, add the oil and heat for 2-3 minutes. Add the onions and sauté until light pink. Add the tomatoes and cook until soft. Now add the remaining Haleem masala, 1 tsp ginger-garlic paste, and mutton. Roast for 2-3 minutes.
6. Stir in the yoghurt, red chilli powder, ½ cup water and season to taste with salt. Lock the lid and cook for 6 whistles, or 15-18 minutes. Remove from heat and let the pressure release.
7. Open the lid and simmer over low heat to ensure the mutton is tender. Remove from heat.
8. Now heat a cooking pot for 2-3 minutes and combine the prepared dal mixture and mutton. Stir well and add the ground whole spices. Cover the pot with a lid and cook for 10 minutes until the flavours have combined well.

TO MAKE THE TEMPERING:

9. Heat the oil in a small wok over medium heat. Add the sliced onion and stir-fry until golden brown. Pour over the khichda. Garnish with green chillies, ginger, lime wedges, and fried onions. Serve hot as is or with steamed rice.

SERVES: **4-6**

KEEMA KHICHDI

Mixed-grain stew with minced mutton

INGREDIENTS

250 g rice

50 g black gram (*urad chilka*)

100 ml refined oil

2 medium-sized onions, sliced

½ kg minced mutton/lamb (*keema*), hand-ground

1 Tbsp ginger-garlic paste (p. 21)

2 medium-sized tomatoes, chopped

Salt, to taste

1 tsp coriander (*dhaniya*) powder

1 tsp red chilli (*lal mirch*) powder

1 tsp turmeric (*haldi*) powder

1 tsp garam masala (p. 16)

2 Tbsp yoghurt (*dahi*)

4 green chillies (*hari mirch*), chopped (optional)

2 tsp ghee

METHOD

1. Rinse the rice and black gram thoroughly. Soak them together in 3 cups of water for 30 minutes.
2. In a pressure cooker over medium heat, add the oil and heat for 2-3 minutes. Add the sliced onions and sauté until they brown.
3. Add the keema, ginger-garlic paste, and tomatoes. Sauté for 2-3 minutes. Season to taste with salt.
4. Stir in the coriander powder, red chilli powder, turmeric and garam masala, and simmer for 8-10 minutes.
5. Add the yoghurt and if you prefer it spicy, add the green chillies.
6. Lock the lid in place and cook over medium heat for 3-4 whistles. This should take around 10-12 minutes. Remove from heat and let the pressure release.
7. Open the lid and return the cooker over medium heat. Simmer for 5 minutes, stirring occasionally.
8. Now add 400 ml water to the mixture and bring to a boil over high heat.
9. Add the soaked rice and dal and lock the lid. Pressure cook for 4 whistles. This should take around 12 minutes.
10. Reduce the heat to low and continue cooking (without opening the lid) for another 10 minutes.
11. Remove from heat and let the pressure release. Before serving, drizzle with ghee and serve hot with yoghurt and green chutney (p. 23).

COOKING TIME: **60 MINUTES**

SERVES: **6-8**

KOFTA BIRYANI

Flavourful biryani layered with minced mutton balls

INGREDIENTS

FOR THE KOFTA:

500 g minced mutton/lamb (*keema*), machine ground

½ cup brown onion

1 g fresh coriander (*dhaniya*), chopped

1 g mint (*pudina*) leaves, chopped

½ tsp red chilli (*lal mirch*) powder

2-4 green chilli (*hari mirch*), chopped

1 tsp garam masala (p. 16)

Salt, to taste

½ tsp gram flour (*besan*), roasted

1 tsp ginger-garlic paste (p. 21)

300 ml refined oil, for frying

FOR THE RICE:

400 g rice

Salt, to taste

100 ml refined oil

1 onion, sliced

2-3 green cardamom (*hari elaichi*) pods

1-2 bay leaves (*tej patta*)

3-5 cloves (*laung*)

2-3 green chillies (*hari mirch*), chopped

1 tsp ginger-garlic paste (p. 21)

1 tsp red chilli (*lal mirch*) powder

½ tsp turmeric (*haldi*) powder

½ cup yoghurt (*dahi*), beaten

½ tsp vetiver (*kewra*) water

1 Tbsp fried onions

COOKING TIME: **90 MINUTES**

METHOD

TO MAKE THE KOFTA:

1. In a large bowl, combine all the kofta ingredients (except oil) and mix, so that the meat marinates well. Rest for 30 minutes.
2. Transfer the marinated meat into a mixer-grinder. Grind over medium setting for 2-3 minutes.
3. Transfer the kofta mixture into a bowl and knead into a dough. Wet your palms and divide into equal lemon-sized balls.
4. Heat the oil in a heavy-bottomed pan for 2-3 minutes over high heat. Reduce the heat to medium and in batches, deep fry the koftas until golden brown. Set aside.

TO MAKE THE BIRYANI:

5. Rinse the rice well for a couple of times until the water runs clear of starch.
6. In a cooking pot over medium heat, add 1 litre water and bring to a boil. Add the rice and 1 tsp salt; cook for 5-6 minutes until the rice is almost cooked. Drain any excess water, saving 4 tablespoons of rice water.
7. In a large pot over high heat, heat the oil for 2-3 minutes. Reduce the heat to medium and add onions. Sauté them until brown.
8. Add the green cardamom, bay leaves, cloves, green chillies, ginger-garlic paste, red chilli powder, turmeric, and season to taste with salt. Stir well to combine.
9. Now add the yoghurt and cook, stirring frequently, until the oil separates.
10. Add the prepared koftas into the gravy and simmer for 2-3 minutes to ensure the koftas are completely covered in the gravy. Add the vetiver water.
11. Fold in the rice, fried onions, and the reserved rice water into the pot. Cover with a lid and cook over medium heat for 10-15 minutes. If using food colour, add now.
12. Remove from heat and serve with yoghurt.

SERVES: **4-6**

MUTTON HALEEM

Slow-cooked mutton and grain stew

INGREDIENTS

150 g wheat
50 g barley
10 g rice
10 g yellow mung (*moong dhuli dal*)
10 g red lentils (*masoor dal*)
10 g Bengal gram (*chana dal*)
10 g split pigeon peas (*toor dal*)
10 g black lentils (*urad dal*)
1 tsp garam masala (p. 16)
4-5 garlic cloves, minced
4 bay leaves (*tej patta*)
1 tsp cumin (*jeera*) powder
1½ tsp coriander (*dhaniya*) powder
½ tsp turmeric (*haldi*) powder
1 tsp red chilli (*lal mirch*) powder
Salt, to taste
1 cup oil
1 kg boneless mutton/lamb
½ tsp *kababchini* powder (store bought)
2 (1") pieces ginger, julienned
4 tsp fried onions
4-5 green chillies (*hari mirch*), chopped
1 lemon, cut into slices or wedges

COOKING TIME: **90 MINUTES**

METHOD

1. Soak the wheat, barley, rice, moong dhuli dal, masoor dal, chana dal, toor dal, and urad dal in 2 litres water for about 8 hours or overnight. Drain excess water.
2. In a large pot over high heat, combine 2 litres of water with the soaked grains and lentils. Add the garam masala, garlic, bay leaves, cumin powder, coriander powder, turmeric, and red chilli powder. Season to taste with salt. Bring to a boil and simmer for 45 minutes or until the grains and lentils are cooked through. Remove from heat and let cool.
3. Now transfer to a mixer-grinder and blend over medium setting to make a smooth paste. Set aside.
4. Heat ½ cup oil in a pressure cooker over high heat. Add the mutton and roast it for about 20-25 minutes until browned. Now add 2 cups of water and lock the lid in place. Pressure cook for 3-4 whistles. Remove from heat and let the pressure release.
5. Open the lid and check the mutton. If it is not tender, pressure cook for 2 more whistles. Once tender, allow it to cool and then blend it in a mixer-grinder over medium setting to make a thick paste.
6. In a wok over medium heat, combine the mutton mixture with the grain and lentil paste to achieve a thick pasty consistency. Add the *kababchini* powder and combine well.
7. For tempering, heat the remaining oil (½ cup) in a fry pan over medium heat. Add the ginger, fried onions, and green chillies. Pour half the tempering over the haleem.
8. Remove from heat and garnish with the remaining tempering ingredients and lemon wedges at the time of serving. The dish can be served as is or with sheermal (p. 161).

SERVES: **7-8**

VEG PULAO

Fragrant rice with assorted vegetables

INGREDIENTS

500 g basmati rice

1 small cinnamon (*dal chini*) stick

½ tsp green cardamom pods (*hari elaichi*)

Pinch of mace (*javitri*) powder

2-3 green chillies (*hari mirch*)

Salt, to taste

240 ml refined oil

1 medium-sized onion, sliced

2 tsp ginger-garlic paste (p. 21)

½ tsp turmeric (*haldi*) powder

½ tsp red chilli (*lal mirch*) powder

100 g cauliflower florets

100 g carrots, diced

100 g green beans, chopped

100 g peas

Mint (*pudina*) leaves, to garnish

METHOD

1. Rinse the rice well for a couple of times until the water runs clear of starch. Soak in 2 litres water for 30 minutes. Gently drain.
2. In a large cooking pot over high heat, add 2 litres of water and bring to a boil. Add the rice along with cinnamon, cardamom, mace powder, and green chillies. Season to taste with salt. Cook for 10-12 minutes. Drain the rice in a colander and collect the excess water separately.
3. In another large pot, heat the oil over high heat for 2 minutes. Add the sliced onions and sauté them until brown.
4. Reduce the heat to medium and add the ginger-garlic paste, turmeric, and red chilli powder.
5. Now add all the vegetables and sauté for 3-4 minutes.
6. Add the boiled rice and 2 tablespoons of the reserved rice water. Combine gently, ensuring the rice grains don't break.
7. Cover the pot with a lid and cook for 2-3 minutes.
8. Remove from heat. Garnish with mint leaves and serve with yoghurt.

COOKING TIME: **60 MINUTES**

SERVES: **3-4**

CHANA DAL KI KHICHDI

A comforting blend of rice and lentils

INGREDIENTS

1 cup basmati rice

1 cup Bengal gram (*chana dal*)

50 ml refined oil

1 Tbsp cumin seeds (*jeera sabut*)

½ Tbsp fennel seeds (*saunf*)

2 Tbsp grated ginger

1 large onion, sliced

4-5 garlic cloves, minced

Salt, to taste

½ Tbsp red chilli powder

10 g fresh coriander (*dhaniya*), chopped

METHOD

1. Rinse the rice well for a couple of times until the water runs clear of starch. Soak in ½ litre water for 20-25 minutes. Drain gently.
2. Rinse the dal for a couple of times and set aside.
3. Heat the oil in a large pot over medium heat. Once the oil turns smoky, add the cumin seeds, fennel seeds, and ginger. Sauté for 2-3 minutes.
4. Add the sliced onions, minced garlic and sauté until the onions turn translucent.
5. Season to taste with salt and add the red chilli powder.
6. Now add the dal and 2 cups of water. Simmer for 5 minutes, stirring continuously.
7. Cover the pot with a lid and cook for 30 minutes over low heat until the dal is tender.
8. Pour 4 cups of water and add the rice.
9. Cover the pot with a lid and cook for 30 minutes until the water is absorbed and the dal and rice soften, stirring occasionally.
10. Remove from heat. Garnish with coriander and serve with yoghurt and pickles of choice.

COOKING TIME: **40-45 MINUTES**

SERVES: **4-5**

CHAPPATI

Light flat bread

INGREDIENTS

500 g whole-wheat flour (*atta*)

½ tsp salt

Water, to knead the dough

15 g ghee

1 tsp carom seeds (*ajwain*)*

*1 tsp carom seeds (ajwain) can be added to the same recipe to make Ajwain chappatis.

METHOD

1. In a mixing bowl, combine the wheat flour, carom seeds (if making *ajwain* chappatis), and salt with 1-1½ cups of water. Mix well.
2. Knead the mixture to make a smooth, soft dough.
3. Divide the dough into 10-12 equal roundels.
4. Flatten one roundel slightly before rolling it with a rolling pin over a board into flat roti.
5. Heat the griddle over medium heat.
6. Once hot, place the chappati on the griddle and cook on both sides until light brown.
7. When ready, remove from the griddle and drizzle with ghee. Repeat the process to make more rotis.
8. Serve hot with a main dish of your choice.

COOKING TIME: **30 MINUTES**

SERVES: **4**

SESAME NAAN

Soft, fluffy bread topped with sesame seeds

INGREDIENTS

1 kg all-purpose flour (*maida*)

250 g white sesame seeds (*safed til*) + more to sprinkle on top

1 Tbsp yeast

½ tsp salt

Water, to knead the dough

2 eggs, beaten

100 g butter

METHOD

1. In a mixing bowl, combine all the ingredients except butter with 2-3 cups of water. Mix well.
2. Knead the mixture into a soft and stretchy dough. Do not over knead as this will harden the naans. Cover the bowl with a moist muslin cloth and rest for 2 hours.
3. Divide the dough into 10-12 equal roundels. Sprinkle 1 tablespoon of sesame seeds over all the roundels.
4. Flatten one roundel gently and sprinkle flour over it. Slightly flour the rolling top/area as well. Roll it with a rolling pin into flat naans of a preferred size.
5. Heat a cast iron pan over high heat.
6. Gently place the naan in the pan and sprinkle some more sesame seeds on top.
7. Cook for a minute and then flip the pan on the gas stove and cook for 2-3 minutes.
8. Flip the pan again and scrape the naan with a flat ladle. Butter the naans using a brush and repeat the process to make more naans.
9. Serve hot with a main dish of your choice.

COOKING TIME: **60 MINUTES**

SERVES: **6**

TANDOORI ROTI

Charred, soft bread

INGREDIENTS

1 kg wheat flour (*atta*)

1 Tbsp baking soda

½ tsp salt

Water, to knead the dough

COOKING TIME: **60 MINUTES**

METHOD

1. In a mixing bowl, combine all the ingredients with 2-3 cups of water. Mix well.
2. Knead the mixture into a soft dough.
3. Divide the dough into 10-12 equal roundels.
4. Flatten one roundel slightly and sprinkle flour over it. Roll it with a rolling pin over a board into flat rotis of a preferred size. Don't roll them too thin. Tandoori roti should be a little thick.
5. Add it to a griddle and flip over when done. Each side should take 2-3 minutes until done.
6. When ready, remove from heat. Repeat the process to make more rotis.
7. Serve hot with a main dish of your choice.

SERVES: **6-8**

ROOMALI ROTI

Thin, soft and stretchy roti, perfect for wraps

INGREDIENTS

1 tsp salt, or to taste

1 cup water

500 g all-purpose flour (*maida*) + 50 g for dusting

½ tsp sugar

30 ml refined oil

1 egg

¾ cup warm milk

METHOD

1. Add 1 tsp salt into 1 cup of water.
2. In a mixing bowl, combine the maida, salt water, sugar, oil, egg and mix well.
3. Knead the mixture for 15 minutes to make a soft dough by slowly pouring in warm milk, little by little. Grease the dough with a little oil and cover with a moist muslin cloth. Rest for 15 minutes.
4. Divide the dough into 6-7 equal roundels.
5. Flatten one roundel slightly and dust maida over it. Roll it as thin and stretchy as possible with a rolling pin into flat rotis of a preferred size.
6. Heat a wok for 2 minutes over high heat. Sprinkle some water and let it sizzle. Unroll the roti onto the wok.
7. When it bubbles, use a soft cloth to flip it gently and press it down.
8. When golden spots start appearing, remove from heat. Repeat the process to make more rotis.
9. Serve hot with a main dish of your choice.

COOKING TIME: **90 MINUTES**

SERVES: **6-7**

METHI CHAPPATI

Rotis packed with fenugreek

INGREDIENTS

1 kg fenugreek leaves without stems (*methi*), coarsely chopped

500 g wheat flour (*atta*)

1 Tbsp salt

Water, to knead the dough

30 ml refined oil

Butter, as needed

METHOD

1. In a mixing bowl, combine the fenugreek leaves, wheat flour and salt with 2-3 cups of water.
2. Knead the mixture into a soft dough.
3. Divide the dough into 12-14 equal-sized roundels.
4. Flatten one roundel slightly before rolling it with a rolling pin over a board into flat circles.
5. Heat the griddle over medium heat. Add 1-2 tsp oil.
6. Place the roti on the hot griddle and cook on both sides until brown. Each side should take 1-2 minutes.
7. When ready, remove from heat and drizzle with butter. Repeat the process with the other roundels.
8. Serve hot with a main dish of your choice and yoghurt.

COOKING TIME: **35-40 MINUTES**

SERVES: **6-8**

BESAN ROTI

Spiced gram flour chappatis

INGREDIENTS

½ kg gram flour (*besan*)

3 Tbsp wheat flour (*atta*)

½ tsp carom seeds (*ajwain*)

5 g fresh coriander (*dhaniya*), finely chopped

2 green chillies (*hari mirch*), finely chopped

1 (1") piece ginger, chopped

Salt, to taste

1 small onion, finely chopped

Water, to knead the dough

30 ml refined oil

Butter, as needed

METHOD

1. In a mixing bowl, combine all the ingredients (except oil and butter) with 2-3 cups of water. Mix well.
2. Knead the mixture to make a soft dough.
3. Divide the dough into 8-10 equal roundels.
4. Flatten one roundel slightly before rolling it with a rolling pin over a board into flat circles.
5. Heat the griddle over medium heat and add ½ Tbsp oil.
6. Gently place the roti on the griddle and cook on both sides, adding ½ Tbsp oil for the other side. Each side should take about a minute.
7. When ready, remove from heat and drizzle with butter. Repeat the process with the other roundels.
8. Serve hot with a main dish of your choice.

COOKING TIME: **35-40 MINUTES**

SERVES: **6-8**

BATHUA ROTI

Rotis made with bathua leaves served with red chutney

INGREDIENTS

FOR THE RED CHUTNEY:

8 dry red chillies (*lal mirch sookhi*)

4 garlic cloves

Salt, to taste

½ cup water

FOR THE ROTI:

½ kg chenopodium (*bathua*), boil without water and cool it and grind

300 g wheat flour (*atta*)

½ Tbsp caraway (*kaala jeera*)

Salt, to taste

2 Tbsp butter

METHOD

TO MAKE THE CHUTNEY:

1. In a mixer-grinder, add the dry red chillies, garlic, salt, and ½ cup water and grind at medium setting for 2-3 minutes to make a coarse paste. Transfer the chutney into a small bowl.

TO MAKE THE ROTI:

2. In a cooking pot over high heat, add the bathua leaves and heat for 10 minutes. Once done, remove from heat and set aside to cool.
3. Transfer the leaves to a mixer-grinder. Grind the bathua at medium setting for 2-3 minutes until coarsely powdered.
4. In a large mixing bowl, combine the wheat flour and ground bathua, and mix well using your hand. Season to taste with salt and add caraway seeds. You can add a splash of water, if needed.
5. Knead the mixture to a soft dough. Add 1 Tbsp chutney to the dough, and knead it until mixed well. Rest for 15-20 minutes.
6. Divide the dough into 10-12 equal roundels.
7. Flatten one roundel slightly before rolling it with a rolling pin over a board into flat rotis.
8. Heat the griddle over medium heat. Place the roti on the hot griddle and cook on both sides until brown. Each side should take about a minute to be done.
9. When ready, remove from heat and drizzle with butter. Repeat the process to make more rotis.
10. Serve hot with red chutney.

COOKING TIME: **30 MINUTES**

SERVES: **6-8**

SHEERMAL

Traditional sweet bread

INGREDIENTS

4-5 strands saffron (*kesar*)

1 cup warm milk

1 cup all-purpose flour (*maida*)

¾ cup melted ghee

1½ Tbsp sugar

1 Tbsp salt

2 Tbsp desi ghee

2 drops of poppy seed water (*khuskhus*)

METHOD

1. Soak the saffron in 2 Tbsp warm milk and set aside.
2. In a mixing bowl, combine the maida, melted ghee, sugar, and salt. Slowly pour in warm milk and simultaneously knead the dough, little by little, until a soft dough is formed. Cover with a moist muslin cloth and set aside for 2 hours.
3. Once again, knead the dough and let it rest for 30 minutes.
4. Divide the dough into 2-3 equal roundels of 6 inches with a thickness of ¼ inches. Prick all the roundels with a fork on the surface, ensuring that it does not pass through the dough.
5. Heat the griddle over medium heat.
6. Reduce the heat to low and place the sheermal. Cook until it turns brown. Flip it and cook the other side. Remove from the griddle and add desi ghee on both sides of the sheermal.
7. Smear the sheermal with soaked saffron and khus, one at a time, and cook for a minute.
8. Remove from heat. Baste with ghee and serve hot.

COOKING TIME: **2 HOURS**

SERVES: **6-8**

RAITA

DAHI WADA

Soft white gram dumplings in tangy yoghurt

INGREDIENTS

500 g white gram (*urad daal dhuli*), skinned

1 ltr water

½ Tbsp baking soda (*meetha soda*)

1 (2") piece ginger, finely chopped

250 ml refined oil

4 cups yoghurt (*dahi*)

1 cup milk

Salt, to taste

½ tsp black salt (*kala namak*) powder

1 tsp sugar

½ tsp red chilli (*lal mirch*) powder

1 tsp cumin seeds (*jeera sabut*), roasted and powdered

1 tsp cumin (*jeera*) powder

1 tsp chaat masala (p. 17)

2 Tbsp tamarind paste (p. 23)

METHOD

1. Rinse and soak the skinned white gram in a bowl of water until it is completely submerged for 2 hours. Drain excess water.
2. In a mixer-grinder, add the soaked dal and 2 tablespoons of water and grind at a medium setting for 2-3 minutes to a fine paste, creating a thick batter. To ensure the dumplings are soft, beat the paste using a hand-beater or electric beater until the batter is fluffy.
3. Add the baking soda and ginger, and beat until mixed well. Set aside.
4. In a wok over high heat, add the oil and heat until it starts to simmer. Reduce the heat to medium.
5. Wet your palms and in batches shape the batter into a large lemon-sized ball. Flatten the top and gently drop it into the hot oil. Deep fry over medium heat and then reduce the heat and fry until golden brown on all sides. Use a slotted spoon and drain on kitchen towels. Repeat the process to make more wadas.
6. Transfer the wadas into a bowl of lukewarm water and soak for 15-20 minutes. Hand-squeeze them individually to drain excess water.
7. In a separate bowl, whisk the yoghurt, ensuring that there are no lumps. Add the milk, salt, black salt, sugar and whisk well.
8. Place the wadas in a serving bowl and pour the yoghurt mixture over it until they are covered evenly.
9. Sprinkle the red chilli powder, ground cumin seeds, cumin powder, and chaat masala over the dahi wadas.
10. Pour the tamarind paste over it or serve it separately. The dahi wadas can be served chilled or at room temperature.

COOKING TIME: **90 MINUTES**

SERVES: **4-6**

MAKHANA RAITA

Creamy yoghurt with crunchy fox nuts

INGREDIENTS

500 g yoghurt (*dahi*)

Salt, to taste

1 tsp black salt (*kala namak*)

½ cup milk

100 g fox nuts (*makhana*)

1 tsp cumin seeds (*jeera sabut*), roasted and powdered

1 tsp red chilli (*lal mirch*) powder

METHOD

1. In a large bowl, add the yoghurt, salt, black salt and whisk. Add the milk to ensure there are no lumps and the raita does not thicken.
2. Soak the makhana in water for 5 minutes. Once done, hand-squeeze them to drain excess water. Transfer them to a bowl.
3. Pour the yoghurt mixture over the makhana and mix well.
4. Sprinkle the roasted cumin and red chilli powder over it and serve chilled.

COOKING TIME: **15 MINUTES**

SERVES: **4-5**

ALOO RAITA

Rich yoghurt with spiced potatoes

INGREDIENTS

500 g yoghurt (*dahi*)

Salt, to taste

½ tsp black salt (*kala namak*)

¼ tsp black pepper (*kali mirch*)

½ cup milk

3 medium-sized potatoes, boiled, peeled, and cubed

1 Tbsp oil

1 tsp cumin seeds (*jeera sabut*)

4-5 garlic cloves, chopped

METHOD

1. In a large bowl, combine the yoghurt with salt, black salt, black pepper and whisk well, ensuring that there are no knots, adding milk or water if it is too thick.
2. Add the boiled potatoes and mix gently.
3. Heat the oil in a small pan over medium heat. Add the cumin seeds and garlic. Sauté until aromatic.
4. Remove from heat and pour it over the raita and cover until serving.

COOKING TIME: **20-25 MINUTES**

SERVES: **8-10**

LAUKI RAITA

Yoghurt with grated bottle gourd

INGREDIENTS

2 cups water

Salt, to taste

½ small bottle gourd (*lauki*), grated

500 g yoghurt (*dahi*)

Black salt (*kala namak*), to taste

½ Tbsp cumin seeds (*jeera sabut*), roasted

15 ml refined oil

4-6 garlic cloves, minced

METHOD

1. In a pot over high heat, add 2 cups water and salt, and bring to a boil. Add the grated bottle gourd and let simmer for 5 minutes. Remove from heat. Squeeze out excess water and set aside.
2. Hand-squeeze the gourd to drain excess water and transfer into a bowl.
3. In a large bowl, combine the yoghurt with salt, black salt, and cumin seeds. Whisk well.
4. Add the boiled gourd.
5. Heat the oil in a small pan over medium heat. Add the garlic and sauté until aromatic.
6. Remove from heat and pour it over the raita and cover until serving.

COOKING TIME: **25-30 MINUTES**

SERVES: **8-10**

DAHI PHULKI

Gram flour balls in yoghurt

INGREDIENTS

100 g gram flour (*besan*)

Pinch of baking soda (*meetha soda*)

Salt, to taste

Water, as needed

430 ml refined oil

500 g yoghurt (*dahi*)

1 Tbsp cumin seeds (*jeera sabut*), roasted and powdered (¾ Tbsp for the yoghurt mix and ¼ Tbsp for tempering)

½ tsp black salt (*kala namak*)

4-5 garlic cloves, sliced

METHOD

1. In a large bowl, add the gram flour, baking soda and salt, and make a thick batter by stirring in water as required. Set aside for 10 minutes.
2. In a pot over medium heat, add 2 cups of water and bring to a boil. Set aside to cool for 5 minutes.
3. In a wok over high heat, add 400 ml oil and let it simmer. Reduce the heat to medium.
4. Hand-roll the batter into small lemon-sized balls and deep fry until golden brown. Use a slotted spoon and drain on kitchen towels. Repeat for the entire batter.
5. Simultaneously, in a cooking pot, add 1 litre of water and bring to a boil. Set aside to cool for 5 minutes. Drop the prepared fritters into the hot water, 8-10 at a time, and remove them in 30 seconds. Hand-squeeze each to drain excess water and set aside in a serving bowl.
6. In a separate large bowl, combine the yoghurt with salt, ¾ Tbsp cumin seeds powder, and black salt. Whisk well, ensuring that there are no knots. You can add milk or water if it is too thick.
7. Pour this yoghurt mix over the fritters.
8. In a small pan over medium heat, add 30 ml oil and sauté the remaining cumin seeds and garlic until aromatic.
9. Remove from heat and pour it over the raita and cover until serving.

COOKING TIME: **25-30 MINUTES**

SERVES: **8-10**

DESSERTS

ZARDA

Saffron-infused sweet rice

INGREDIENTS

1 cup basmati rice

60 g ghee

8-10 cashews (*kaju*), halved

8-10 almonds (*badaam*), chopped

1 Tbsp raisins (*kishmish*)

2 Tbsp dry coconut

2 cups sugar

2 pods green cardamom (*hari elaichi*) pods

4 cloves (*laung*)

¼ Tbsp saffron (*kesar*)

¼ Tbsp orange colour

1 ltr water

METHOD

1. Rinse the rice well for a couple of times until the water runs clear of starch. Soak for 30 minutes in 4-5 cups of water. Drain excess water and set aside.
2. In a pot over high heat, add 2 tablespoons of ghee. Once it starts to simmer, reduce the heat to medium.
3. Add the cashews, almonds, raisins and dry coconut, and roast them until golden brown. Use a slotted spoon and drain the roasted dry fruits on kitchen towels. Set aside to cool.
4. In the same pot, now add the remaining ghee, sugar, green cardamom, cloves, saffron, and colour. Add 1 litre water and stir well to combine.
5. Now add the soaked rice and stir well. Cover the pot with a lid.
6. Reduce the heat to low and cook for 10 minutes until the rice is half cooked.
7. In a large pan over medium heat, add 100 g ghee and transfer the contents of the pot into it. Cover the pan and cook until the water dries out and the rice is fully cooked. Remove from heat.
8. Garnish with the roasted dry fruits and nuts. Serve warm or cold.

COOKING TIME: **40-45 MINUTES**

SERVES: **2**

PHIRNI

Creamy rice pudding

INGREDIENTS

250 g rice

2 Tbsp coconut powder

2 ltrs milk

400 g sugar

3-4 green cardamom (*hari elaichi*) pods, powdered

3 Tbsp condensed milk

100 g almonds (*badaam*), slivered

3-4 pistachios (*pista*), roughly chopped

COOKING TIME: **50-60 MINUTES**

METHOD

1. Rinse the rice well for a couple of times until the water runs clear of starch. Soak for 1 hour in enough water to submerge it completely. Gently drain the excess water and spread the rice to dry over a muslin cloth for 1 hour.
2. In a mixer-grinder, add the coconut powder and dried rice together and grind at medium setting to make a coarse powder. Do not grind the rice to a fine powder.
3. In a large pan over high heat, add the milk and bring to a boil. Slowly stir in the powdered coconut and rice mixture to ensure there are no knots. Keep stirring and when it thickens, reduce the heat. Add the sugar and mix well.
4. Once the rice granules are fully cooked and the pudding has thickened, add the powdered cardamom and condensed milk and stir well for 2 minutes. Remove from heat.
5. Transfer to a clay bowl to set. Garnish with a small spoonful of condensed milk, if preferred, and pistachios.
6. Once cool, as it reaches room temprature, cover the bowl with aluminium foil and refrigerate for atleast 4 hours.
7. Serve chilled.

SERVES: **4-5**

SHEER KORMA

Sweet vermicelli pudding

INGREDIENTS

2 ltr milk

300 g sugar

50 g cardamom (*elaichi*) powder

½ can condensed milk

500 g vermicelli (*sevaiyan*)

50 g almond (*badaam*) powder

8-10 almonds (*badaam*), slivered

8-10 cashews (*kaju*), sliced

8-10 raisins (*kishmish*), sliced

METHOD

1. In a cooking pot over high heat, add the milk and sugar and bring to a boil. Simmer until the sugar dissolves completely.
2. Reduce the heat to medium-low and add cardamom powder and condensed milk; stir well. Remove from heat and set aside.
3. In a separate wok over low heat, dry roast the vermicelli until light brown/golden and aromatic.
4. Stir in the milk into the wok and let simmer, stirring frequently. The vermicelli and milk should combine well and thicken. Add the almond powder and mix well.
5. Remove from heat and transfer into a serving bowl. Garnish with slivered almonds, cashews, and raisins. Refrigerate for atleast 4 hours and serve chilled.

COOKING TIME: **30-35 MINUTES**

SERVES: **6-8**

CHANA DAL HALWA

Bengal gram halwa

INGREDIENTS

1 ltr milk

500 g Bengal gram (*chana dal*), washed and rinsed

300 g ghee

300 g sugar

50 g cardamom (*elaichi*) powder

80 g almonds (*badaam*), roughly chopped

80 g cashew nuts (*kaju*), roughly chopped

80 g raisins (*kishmish*), chopped

METHOD

1. In a wok over high heat, add the milk and bring to a boil. Add the Bengal gram and simmer for 20 minutes until the dal softens, stirring frequently. Remove from heat and set aside for 5-7 minutes to cool.
2. Now transfer the dal mixture to a mixer-grinder. Blend at medium setting for 2-3 minutes to a smooth paste. Transfer into a bowl and set aside.
3. In a wok over high heat, add the ghee. Reduce the heat and add the prepared dal paste and cook until it turns brown and aromatic.
4. Add the sugar and cardamom powder and cook until the sugar dissolves. At this stage, the halwa will dry out and the ghee will separate.
5. Remove from heat, garnish with almonds, cashew nuts, and raisins. Serve warm.

COOKING TIME: **40-45 MINUTES**

SERVES: **6-8**

SEVAIYAN KIMAMI

Rich vermicelli pudding

INGREDIENTS

4 cups water

400 g sugar

2-3 cloves (*laung*)

3-4 green cardamom (*hari elaichi*) pods

2 drops vetiver water (*kewra*)

½ Tbsp edible red colour

30 g ghee

500 g vermicelli (*sevaiyan*)

COOKING TIME: **40-45 MINUTES**

METHOD

1. In a medium-sized pan over high heat, add 4 cups of water and sugar. Bring to a boil and simmer for 5 minutes until the sugar dissolves and the mixture reaches a thick, syrupy consistency.
2. Add the cloves, green cardamom, vetiver water, food colour, and stir well. Remove from heat.
3. Heat the ghee in a wok over medium heat. Add the vermicelli and roast until golden brown and aromatic.
4. Now gradually pour the syrup over the vermicelli. Reduce the heat and stirring gently, cook for 8-10 minutes.
5. Garnish with your choice of dry fruits and serve warm.

SERVES: **6-8**

ANDA HALWA

Egg halwa

INGREDIENTS

6 eggs

500 ml milk

200 g ghee

250 g sugar

1 Tbsp cardamom (*elaichi*) powder

80 g almonds (*badaam*), chopped

80 g cashew nuts (*kaju*), chopped

80 g raisins (*kishmish*), chopped

COOKING TIME: **20-25 MINUTES**

METHOD

1. In a large bowl, whisk the eggs with milk.
2. Heat the ghee in a wok over low heat. Add the whisked eggs and cook slowly whilst stirring continuously.
3. Add the sugar, cardamom powder and cook until the sugar dissolves and the halwa thickens and becomes grainy. Remove from heat.
4. Garnish with almonds, raisins, and cashews. Serve warm.

SERVES: **4-6**

SHAHI TUKDA

The royal Indian take on bread pudding

INGREDIENTS

FOR RABRI:

½ tsp saffron

½ tsp vetiver (*kewra*) water

4 cups full-fat milk

3 Tbsp milk powder

2½ cups sugar

10-12 almonds (*badaam*), slivered

15-20 pistachios (*pista*), sliced

FOR SUGAR SYRUP:

½ cup sugar

¼ cup water

4 green cardamom (*hari elaichi*) pods, powdered

FOR PAN-FRYING BREAD:

180 g ghee (30 g per slice of bread)

5-6 slice of milk bread without crust (with a thickness of 1 inch)

2 ltr or 4 cups milk

300 g sugar

50 g almonds (*badaam*) powder

50 g cardamom (*elaichi*) powder

½ can condensed milk

METHOD

1. In a small bowl, dissolve the saffron in vetiver water for 30 minutes.
2. In a deep pan or wok over high heat, bring the milk to a boil and add milk powder. Remove clotted cream and keep adding it back to the milk. Stir and scrape the sides continuously to ensure that the milk does not turn brown. Add the dissolved saffron to the pan.
3. Reduce the heat and let simmer until the milk thickens. Add the sugar and stir until it completely melts.
4. Now add the almonds and pistachios. The milk will thicken further and reach a rabri-like consistency. Remove from heat and set aside.
5. In a flat pan over medium-low heat, heat 1 tablespoon ghee and toast one slice of bread until golden brown. Flip the bread to toast the other side, adding ghee if required. Repeat the step to toast the remaining slices.
6. In a wide bowl, combine sugar, water, and green cardamom. Mix well to get the sugar syrup.
7. Transfer the toasted bread slices into the bowl with the sugar syrup, ensuring they submerge completely. Squeeze any excess syrup with your hands and rest.
8. In a separate flat bowl, layer the prepared rabri at the bottom. Top it with a layer of bread. Repeat the process to layer once more.
9. Refrigerate and serve cold with dried fruits and nuts of your choice.

COOKING TIME: **120 MINUTES**

SERVES: **6-8**

NIMISH

A light, airy dessert made of whipped milk and cream foam

INGREDIENTS

8 cups full-cream raw milk

2 cups cream

1 Tbsp cream of tartar

1 cup caster sugar

1 Tbsp rose water

2 Tbsp pistachios (*pista*), finely sliced

METHOD

1. In a large bowl, combine the milk, cream, and cream of tartar and refrigerate overnight, or for 8 hours.
2. Once cool, add 4 tablespoons of caster sugar and one teaspoon of rose water to the refrigerated bowl and whisk the mixture using an electric beater at high speed until a foamy layer appears on top. Using a large tea strainer, collect the foam from the top and transfer it to a large tray. Keep the tray tilted so the foam stays on one side and the milk collects on the lower side.
3. When the tray is full, spoon the foam into small glass ramekins, sprinkling ½ tsp caster sugar between each layer and on top. At this stage, the foam should have condensed and liquefied.
4. Pour the milk collected in the tray back into the bowl and continue beating and collecting the foam for 2 hours or until no milk remains.
5. Garnish pistachios over each bowl and serve chilled.

COOKING TIME: **2½ HOURS**

SERVES: **4-5**

SOOJI HALWA

Semolina halwa

INGREDIENTS

12-14 almonds (*badaam*)

2½ cups water

¾ cup sugar

470 g ghee

1 cup semolina (*sooji*), dry roasted

COOKING TIME: **30-35 MINUTES**

METHOD

1. In a small bowl, add the almonds and enough hot water to submerge them completely. Allow them to soak for 1 hour. Peel the almonds and cut into thin strips.
2. In a medium-size pan over medium heat, add 2½ cups water and sugar and stir until the sugar dissolves completely. Remove from heat and set aside.
3. In a wok over medium heat, add the ghee and semolina. Roast while stirring for 8-10 minutes until the semolina turns aromatic and light brown.
4. Now gently pour the sugar syrup into the semolina and whisk continuously so that the semolina absorbs the syrup. Stir for 2 minutes until the sooji thickens and the ghee separates.
5. Remove from heat. Garnish with almonds and serve warm.

SERVES: **6-8**

MANGO PHIRNI

Creamy mango pudding

INGREDIENTS

4-5 mangoes, chopped

2 Tbsp custard powder

4½ cups milk

100 g khoya, grated

½ cup sugar

Pinch of edible yellow colour (optional)

¼ cup fresh cream

2 tsp condensed milk

Mango chunks (optional)

METHOD

1. Blend the mangoes in a blender at medium setting to make a thick puree.
2. In a medium-size bowl, combine the custard powder with 1/3 cup of milk, ensuring it is smooth and lump-free.
3. In a large vessel over high heat, bring 4 cups of milk to a boil. Reduce the heat to medium and let simmer.
4. Add the grated khoya and sugar to the simmering milk. Stir until the sugar dissolves completely.
5. Now gently stir in the custard-milk mixture into the milk and cook over medium heat for 2 minutes. Add a pinch of yellow food colour, if desired.
6. Now add the fresh cream and stir well. The consistensy should be thick and creamy.
7. Remove from heat and allow the mixture to cool, and then refrigerate for 2 hours.
8. Once chilled, add the mango puree and condensed milk; whisk well to combine.
9. Top the phirni with mango chunks for added texture, if desired.
10. Serve chilled in clay pots.

COOKING TIME: **40 MINUTES**

SERVES: **4-5**

INDEX

All rights are reserved. No part of this publication may be transmitted or reproduced in any form or by any means without prior permission from the publisher.

First published in India by Roli Books, 2025

© Concept, design and layout: Roli Books
© Introduction & Recipes: Pernia Qureshi
Food photographs by Karishma Karamchandani
Family photographs, courtesy Pernia Qureshi
Cover illustration: Anita Verma

ISBN: 9789392130472

Published in India by Roli Books Pvt Ltd
M-75, Greater Kailash II Market
New Delhi-110 048, India
Phone: +91-11-40682000
Email: info@rolibooks.com
Website: www.rolibooks.com

Printed and bound in India